2nd Workshop on Natural Language Reasoning and Structured Explanations

Bangkok, Thailand
15 August 2024

ISBN: 979-8-3313-0172-9

Printed from e-media with permission by:

Curran Associates, Inc.
57 Morehouse Lane
Red Hook, NY 12571

Some format issues inherent in the e-media version may also appear in this print version.

Printed with permission by Curran Associates, Inc. (2025)

For permission requests, please contact the Association for Computational Linguistics at the address below.

Association for Computational Linguistics
209 N. Eighth Street
Stroudsburg, Pennsylvania 18360

Phone: 1-570-476-8006
Fax: 1-570-476-0860

acl@aclweb.org

Additional copies of this publication are available from:

Curran Associates, Inc.
57 Morehouse Lane
Red Hook, NY 12571 USA
Phone: 845-758-0400
Fax: 845-758-2633
Email: curran@proceedings.com
Web: www.proceedings.com

ACL 2024

2nd Workshop on Natural Language Reasoning and Structured Explanations (@ACL 2024)

Proceedings of the Workshop

August 15, 2024

Association for Computational Linguistics (ACL)
317 Sidney Baker St. S
Suite 400 - 134
Kerrville, TX 78028
USA
Tel: +1-855-225-1962
acl@aclweb.org

Introduction

Welcome to NLRSE, the Second Workshop on Natural Language Reasoning and Structured Explanations, co-located with ACL 2024 in Bangkok, Thailand.

With recent scaling of large pre-trained Transformer language models (LLMs), the scope of feasible NLP tasks has broadened. Significant recent work has focused on tasks that require some kind of natural language reasoning. A trajectory in question answering has led us from extraction-oriented datasets like SQuAD to "multi-hop" reasoning datasets like HotpotQA and StrategyQA. Although LLMs have shown remarkable performance on most NLP tasks, it is often unclear why their answers follow from what they know. To address this gap, a new class of explanation techniques has emerged which play an integral part in structuring the reasoning necessary to solve these datasets. For example, the chain-of-thought paradigm leverages explanations as vehicles for LLMs to mimic human reasoning processes. Entailment trees offer a way to ground multi-step reasoning in a collection of verifiable steps. Frameworks like SayCan bridge high-level planning in language and with low-level action trajectories. As a result, we see a confluence of methods blending explainable machine learning/NLP, classical AI (especially theorem proving), and cognitive science (how do humans structure explanations?). This workshop aims to bring together a diverse set of perspectives from these different traditions and attempt to establish common ground for how these various kinds of explanation structures can tackle a broad class of reasoning problems in natural language and beyond.

A total of 7 papers appear in the proceedings. 40 papers were presented at the workshop itself, with the rest being submitted under two archival options: cross-submissions (Findings papers or those already presented at other venues, such as EMNLP or the ACL main conference), and regular non-archival submissions (unpublished work). The latter went through a normal peer review process. These papers can be found on the NLRSE website: `https://nl-reasoning-workshop.github.io/`

Six papers were featured as oral presentations. These papers represented a selection of strong work that the organizers felt would be of broad interest to workshop participants. In addition, we featured four invited talks: Sherry Wu, Karthik Narasimhan, Thomas Icard, and Lorraine Li.

We are thankful to all reviewers for their help in the selection of the program, for their readiness in engaging in thoughtful discussions about individual papers, and for providing valuable feedback to the authors. We would also like to thank the ACL workshop organizers for all the valuable help and support with organizational aspects of the conference. Finally, we would like to thank all our authors and presenters for making this such an exciting event!

Bhavana Dalvi, Greg Durrett, Peter Jansen, Ben Lipkin, Danilo Ribeiro, Lio Wong, Xi Ye, and Wenting Zhao, NLRSE organizers

Organizing Committee

Organizers

Bhavana Dalvi Mishra, Allen Institute for Artificial Intelligence
Greg Durrett, UT Austin
Peter Jansen, University of Arizona
Ben Lipkin, Massachusetts Institute of Technology
Danilo Neves Ribeiro, Amazon AWS
Lio Wong, Massachusetts Institute of Technology
Xi Ye, UT Austin
Wenting Zhao, Cornell University

Program Committee

Program Chairs

Bhavana Dalvi Mishra, Allen Institute for Artificial Intelligence
Greg Durrett, University of Texas, Austin
Peter Jansen, University of Arizona
Ben Lipkin, Massachusetts Institute of Technology
Danilo Neves Ribeiro, Amazon AWS
Lionel Wong, Massachusetts Institute of Technology
Xi Ye, University of Texas, Austin
Wenting Zhao, Cornell University

Program Committee

Jun Araki, Bosch Research
Jinheon Baek, Korea Advanced Institute of Science & Technology
Kaj Bostrom, University of Texas, Austin
Faeze Brahman, Allen Institute for AI
Justin T Chiu, Cornell University
Yung-Sung Chuang, Massachusetts Institute of Technology
Shahriar Golchin, University of Arizona
Shashank Gupta, Allen Institute for Artificial Intelligence
Naoya Inoue, RIKEN and Japan Advanced Institute of Science and Technology
Uri Katz, Bar-Ilan University
Arun Balajiee Lekshmi Narayanan, University of Pittsburgh
Zhengzhong Liang, Google
Ziqian Luo, Oracle
Bodhisattwa Prasad Majumder, Allen Institute for Artificial Intelligence
Enrique Noriega-Atala, University of Arizona
Yasumasa Onoe, Google
Soumya Sanyal
Zayne Rea Sprague, University of Texas at Austin
Arvind Krishna Sridhar, Qualcomm Inc, QualComm
Oyvind Tafjord, Allen Institute for Artificial Intelligence
Harsh Trivedi, State University of New York, Stony Brook
Hoang Van
Ruoyao Wang, University of Arizona
Anne Wu, Cornell University
Li Zhang
Jiawei Zhou
Bowei Zou, A*STAR

Table of Contents

Program

Tuesday, August 15, 2023

08:00 - 09:00	*Virtual Poster Session*
08:55 - 09:00	*Opening Remarks*
09:00 - 09:45	*Invited Speaker - Sherry Wu*
09:45 - 10:30	*Invited Speaker - Karthik Narasimhan*
10:30 - 11:00	*Break*
11:00 - 11:45	*Invited Speaker - Thomas Icard*
11:45 - 12:30	*Oral Presentations 1*
12:30 - 14:00	*Lunch*
14:00 - 14:45	*Invited Speaker - Lorraine Li*
14:45 - 15:30	*Oral Presentations 2*
15:30 - 16:00	*Break*
16:00 - 17:30	*Poster Session*

GraphReason: Enhancing Reasoning Capabilities of Large Language Models through A Graph-Based Verification Approach

Lang Cao
University of Illinois Urbana-Champaign
Department of Computer Science
langcao2@illinois.edu

Abstract

Large Language Models (LLMs) have showcased impressive reasoning capabilities, particularly when guided by specifically designed prompts in complex reasoning tasks such as math word problems. These models typically solve tasks using a chain-of-thought approach, which not only bolsters their reasoning abilities but also provides valuable insights into their problem-solving process. However, there is still significant room for enhancing the reasoning abilities of LLMs. Some studies suggest that the integration of an LLM output verifier can boost reasoning accuracy without necessitating additional model training. In this paper, we follow these studies and introduce a novel graph-based method to further augment the reasoning capabilities of LLMs. We posit that multiple solutions to a reasoning task, generated by an LLM, can be represented as a reasoning graph due to the logical connections between intermediate steps from different reasoning paths. Therefore, we propose the Reasoning Graph Verifier (GraphReason) to analyze and verify the solutions generated by LLMs. By evaluating these graphs, models can yield more accurate and reliable results.Our experimental results show that our graph-based verification method not only significantly enhances the reasoning abilities of LLMs but also outperforms existing verifier methods in terms of improving these models' reasoning performance.

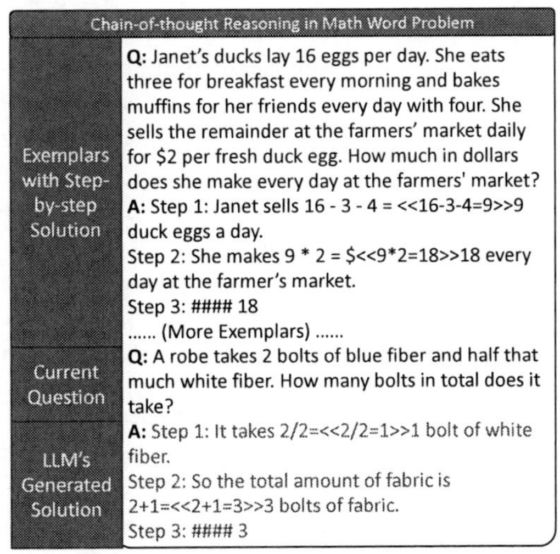

Figure 1: An example of chain-of-thought reasoning in a math word problem, using data from the GSM8K dataset. Large language models learn from exemplars that provide step-by-step solutions, subsequently generating their reasoning path for the current question.

1 Introduction

Large Language Models (LLMs) have demonstrated exceptional capabilities in a variety of human tasks (Zhao et al., 2023). Among the many abilities LLMs possess, their reasoning capacity is of paramount importance (Kojima et al., 2023; Huang and Chang, 2023). This has been substantiated by recent progresses (Wei et al., 2022; Zhou et al., 2023; Lampinen et al., 2022a). Equipped with the ability to reason, especially in a multi-step manner, LLMs can decompose complex problems into simpler tasks, thereby facilitating their resolution. In everyday life, many complex tasks typically require multi-step solutions. A prime example of a reasoning task is arithmetic reasoning, also known as solving math word problems (Zhang et al., 2019). These math word problems represent simplified versions of complex real-life situations.

The reasoning ability is inherent in Large Language Models (LLMs), but it necessitates specific methods for manifestation. To activate the robust reasoning capability of LLMs, the use of specially designed prompts should be considered. Numerous methods have been proposed to tap into this potential, among which chain-of-thought reasoning (Wei et al., 2022) and in-context learning (Lampinen et al., 2022b) are two notable approaches. Chain-of-thought reasoning can elucidate the reasoning paths during the process. In-context learning fur-

Proceedings of the 2nd Workshop on Natural Language Reasoning and Structured Explanations (@ACL 2024), pages 1–12
August 15, 2024

nishes LLMs with exemplary cases, thereby enabling them to learn from and simulate these examples for improved results. In the arithmetic reasoning scenario, GPT-4 can achieve an accuracy of 92% on the GSM8K dataset using 5-shot chain-of-thought prompts (Cobbe et al., 2021a). This represents a level of difficulty that a bright middle school student should be capable of handling. As depicted in Figure 1, this illustrates a multi-step arithmetic reasoning process in LLMs.

In addition to further training of LLMs and prompt design, some methods have been proposed to enhance the reasoning capabilities of LLMs from the perspective of output verification. The primary idea is to have LLMs generate reasoning paths multiple times, and then design a verifier to evaluate these paths and deliver the final results. (Wang et al., 2023) introduces the concept of *self-consistency*, based on the intuition that a complex reasoning problem usually allows for multiple thought processes, all leading to a unique correct answer. (Li et al., 2023) also proposes *All Roads Lead to Rome*, which introduces a step-aware verifier to analyze reasoning paths not just through the entire path, but at every step. However, both methods treat each reasoning path as an independent entity and do not consider the potential interrelation and interaction between different reasoning paths. Once reasoning paths are disassembled into steps, intermediate steps from one path may bear reasoning relations to other reasoning paths. These methods do not perceive all LLM outputs for a given input as a collective entity, thereby failing to analyze the internal relations of all candidate paths in depth.

Inspired by these observations, we propose **Reasoning Graph** Verifier (`GraphReason`) in this paper. We posit that reasoning paths of one question can form reasoning graphs, where similar intermediate reasoning steps can be merged into the same node. With a graph structure, we can more effectively model and capture the reasoning logic between intermediate steps from different reasoning paths. Specifically, we first construct a reasoning graph based on all outputs from LLMs, and then train a verifier to learn the relationship between the graph structure and the final answer. During the prediction stage, we process the data in the same way as in the training stage, and use the verifier to evaluate each reasoning graph. We then select the reasoning graph with the highest score, using its answer as the final answer. To the best of our knowledge, we are the first to approach reasoning logic of LLMs from a graph perspective. We conduct extensive experiments to demonstrate the improvements over the original LLMs, and show that our method outperforms other verifiers.

In summary, our contributions are as follows:

- We propose a graph-based verification method, `GraphReason`, aimed at significantly enhancing the reasoning capabilities of large language models without the need for additional training of LLMs.
- We establish an arithmetic reasoning benchmark using three Math Word Problem datasets to illustrate the fundamental reasoning performance of large language models, and to provide a fair comparison of the performance of various existing verifiers.
- Our experimental results indicate that the method proposed in this paper outperforms other enhancement methods. We also provide an extensive analysis of the limitations and future potential of `GraphReason`.

2 Related Works

Reasoning of Fine-tuning Models has been extensively studied. It focuses on addressing reasoning tasks using a general sequence-to-sequence approach, enhanced by reasoning-aware pre-training or fine-tuning of language models. (Cobbe et al., 2021a) proposed training a verifier to rank solutions sampled from fine-tuned language models. (Yoran et al., 2022; Wang et al., 2022) suggested equipping language models with reasoning abilities by generating training examples with human-designed templates. (Pi et al., 2022) proposed injecting reasoning capabilities into language models by continually pre-training on program execution data.

Several studies have focused on imbuing PLM with reasoning ability for specific tasks, such as arithmetic reasoning (Cobbe et al., 2021a; Miao et al., 2020; Patel et al., 2021), commonsense reasoning (Talmor et al., 2019), and inductive reasoning (Sinha et al., 2019). For instance, various strategies have been proposed to improve language models' performance on arithmetic reasoning tasks, often referred to as math word problems. (Xie and Sun, 2019) proposed a tree-structured decoder to generate an equation tree, while (Zhang et al., 2020) applied graph convolutional networks to extract relationships of quantities in math problems. (Li et al., 2022) used contrastive learning to better learn patterns in math word problems. However, (Valmeekam et al., 2023; Rae et al., 2022) suggested that reasoning, particularly multi-step reasoning, is often a weakness in language models and other NLP models.

Reasoning of Large Language Models has garnered significant attention and demonstrated immense potential. Recent advancements in LLMs suggest that the ability for multi-step reasoning is already embedded within these large-scale models (Kojima et al., 2023; Huang and Chang, 2023), such as PaLM (Chowdhery et al., 2022), GPT-4 (OpenAI, 2023). Therefore, providing an adequate prompt is sufficient to utilize this reasoning ability. For example, the prompting method proposed by (Kojima et al., 2023; Wei et al., 2022), which is based on a chain-of-thought, could aid LLMs in generating text with arithmetic reasoning and common factual knowledge. Following (Wei et al., 2022), experiments on current language models demonstrated that chain-of-thought prompting could enhance the accuracy of solving math problems from 18% to 57%. (Lampinen et al., 2022b) included explanations in the in-context examples and tested the influence of explanations by evaluating the score between *explain-then-predict* and *predict-then-explain*. Moreover, (Zhou et al., 2023) suggested a two-stage prompting strategy, *least-to-most* prompting, which breaks down a complex problem into a series of subproblems and solves them step-by-step. (Li et al., 2023) proposed sampling multiple times from diverse prompts to enhance the variety of responses.

In addition to designing prompts, adopting additional strategies like verifier has contributed to enhancing the performance of reasoning abilities of large language models. For instance, (Wang et al., 2023) proposes *self-consistency*, which involves sampling different reasoning paths from the language model, and then returning the most consistent final answer via majority voting. (Li et al., 2023) used a step-aware voting verifier to enhance the reasoning ability of LLMs from two perspectives. These methods strive to augment the reasoning abilities or yield superior reasoning results without necessitating additional training of LLMs. Our work continues this research direction, with a specific focus on developing a novel graph-based verifier to boost the reasoning capabilities of LLMs.

3 Methodology

3.1 GraphReason Framework

Problem 1 (Reasoning to Solve Problems) *Given a set of n math word problems $\mathbf{Q} = \{Q_1, Q_2, ..., Q_n\}$, where each Q_i is represented by the text description of a single math word problem, the goal of reasoning to solve math word problems is to generate the answers $\mathbf{A} = \{A_1, A_2, ..., A_n\}$ for these problems. Here, each A_i represents the generated text of the corresponding answer. During the process of large language models generating answers, a set of n reasoning paths for solutions $\mathbf{S} = \{S_1, S_2, ..., S_n\}$ is also produced. Each solution S_i is represented as $S_i = \{Q, Step_1, Step_2, ..., Step_l, A\}$, where each $Step_i$ denotes the intermediate steps in the step-by-step solutions.*

We propose GraphReason to verify the solutions generated by LLMs in order to improve the final answer accuracy. This method is a graph-based verification technique that analyzes reasoning paths from generated solutions from a graph perspective. The final answer is obtained without modifying the original LLMs, functioning much like a plugin. As illustrated in Figure 2, there are two steps in the training stage: *Graph Construction* and *Graph Classification*. In the *Graph Construction* step, we obtain the generated solution from LLMs with the specific designed prompt and group them according to their final answers. We split reasoning paths by steps and then merge intermediate steps with identical expression to form reasoning graphs. In the *Graph Classification* step, we classify these reasoning graphs with the additional feature of the sum of scores from the *base verifier* to train the integrated verifier model. In the prediction stage, the candidate solutions are first generated by LLMs. We process them in the same manner as in the training stage, then we use trained verifier to evaluate the scores of each candidate solution. The best solution, denoted by the highest score, is selected as the final predicted answer. We will now provide a detailed introduction to the entire process.

3.2 Prompt Design

To improve the output of Language Models (LLMs) in providing solutions, it is essential to design effective prompts. We incorporate chain-of-thought and in-context learning to enable LLMs to generate step-by-step answers for math word problems. The language models generate output $\mathbf{y}$ based on the

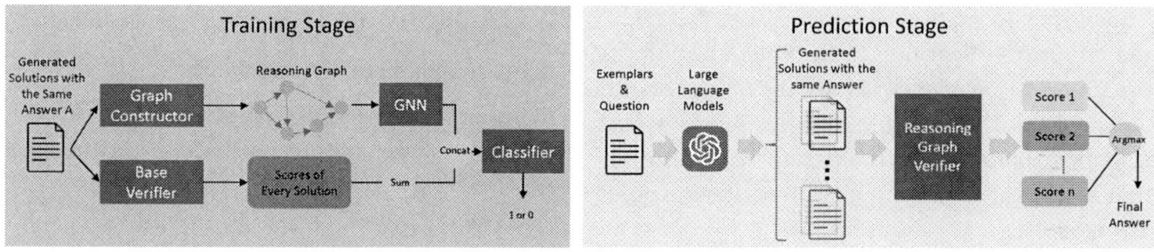

Figure 2: The framework of GraphReason. In the training stage, GraphReason processes generated solutions from LLMs to construct reasoning graphs, and then trains a verifier to judge them according to graph classification. In the prediction stage, GraphReason evaluates candidate solutions to assign a score, and selects the solution with the highest score as the final answer.

input $\mathbf{x}$ using the following equation:

$$p(\mathbf{y}|C, \mathbf{x}) = \prod_{t=1}^{|\mathbf{y}|} p_{LM}(\mathbf{y}_t|C, \mathbf{x}, \mathbf{y} < t), \quad (1)$$

where, C represents the input provided to the LLMs prior to the current math word problem's question. C is a concatenation of k exemplars, denoted as:

$$C = [(Q_1, S_1, A_1); (Q_2, S_2, A_2), ...; (Q_k, S_k, A_k)], \quad (2)$$

where, Q_i represents the question, S_i represents the intermediate steps of the solution, and A_i represents the answer. We set k to five in this study, resulting in a prompt that consists of five question-answer pairs sampled from the training split of a math word problem dataset. Therefore, the prompt can be denoted as:

$$\textbf{Prompt} = [C; Q], \quad (3)$$

where Q represents the question of the current math word problem.

Using a greedy decoding approach to sample one output from LLMs may not be robust. It can lead to instability and occasional errors. To address this, (Wang et al., 2023) propose the concept of *self-consistency*. This approach involves sampling different reasoning paths from the language model and then selecting the most consistent final answer through majority voting. Instead of using greedy decoding to sample only once and verify, they utilize sampling decoding to sample N_1 times. We also follow the idea presented by (Li et al., 2023) in their work named *All Roads Lead to Rome*. This approach involves generating N_2 diverse prompts for LLMs to produce multiple outputs. By employing multiple sampling decodes on diverse prompts, we can obtain generated solutions from different sources. Specifically, we obtain $N = N_1 \times N_2$ diverse reasoning paths for each question. In our main experiments, we set $N_1 = 10$ and $N_2 = 3$. These solutions will be further processed and verified using our designed verifier.

3.3 Reasoning Graph Construction

After generating multiple solutions for a question, it becomes necessary to construct reasoning graphs based on the reasoning paths taken by these solutions.

As shown in Figure 3, we begin by grouping all the generated solutions for a particular question according to their final answer. Since these solutions originate from the same question, their reasoning paths will share the same starting point. Similarly, solutions with the same final answer will have the same endpoint, as their reasoning paths converge. Therefore, a group of generated solutions with the same final answer can form a reasoning graph with a uniform start node (question node) and end node (answer node). We define this division process as follows:

$$\mathbf{S} = \{S_{A_1}, S_{A_2}, ..., S_{A_n}\}, \quad (4)$$

where $\mathbf{S}$ represents the set of generated solutions for a question, and $S_{A_i} = \{S_1, S_2, ..., S_m\}$ is the subset of generated solutions that all have the same final answer A_i.

For each subset of generated solutions S_{A_i}, we construct a reasoning graph. This construction is motivated by the understanding that each step in the reasoning path of a generated solution does not exist in isolation from the other solutions. The steps from one solution's reasoning path can impact the steps from another solution, enhancing the overall reasoning process. We utilize the graph structure to model and capture these relationships between steps from different solutions. As the different reasoning paths can benefit each other, we construct

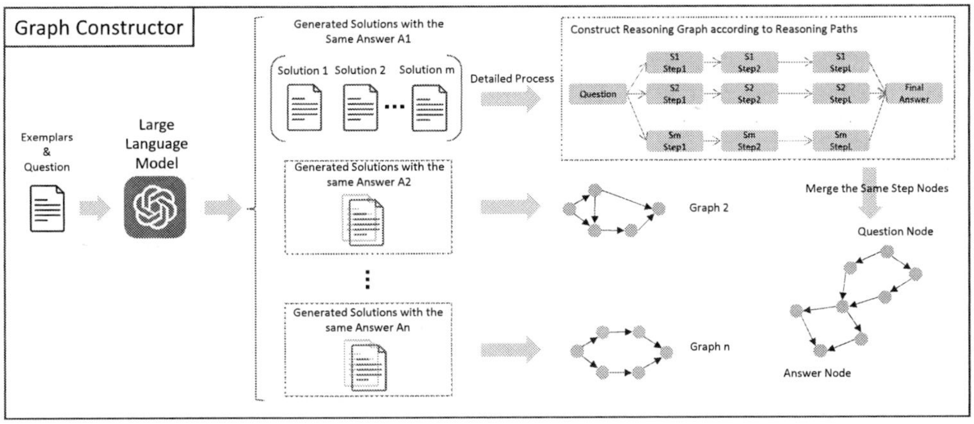

Figure 3: The graph constructor in GraphReason. We detail the process of transforming 'Generated Solutions with the Same Answer A1' to 'Graph 1'.

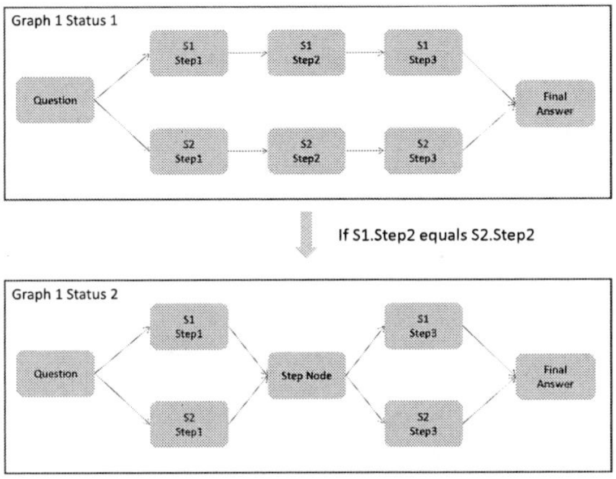

Figure 4: The process of reasoning graph construction. The primary operation here is the merging of identical intermediate steps in reasoning paths into a single graph node.

a reasoning graph to link these paths together. As shown in Figure 4, the primary operation here is the merging of identical intermediate nodes in reasoning paths into a single graph node. We first compare the reasoning steps from any two solution reasoning paths. If they have the same intermediate steps of arithmetic expression, we merge them into the same node, and if they differ, we do not. For reasoning math word problems here, we define reasoning steps as the current arithmetic expression without other language text in the current reasoning step for clarity. It can help us simplify construction of reasoning graphs in the reasoning task. The detailed algorithm for constructing a reasoning graph is shown in Algorithm 1.

The generated solutions, divided by their final answers $\{S_{A_1}, S_{A_2}, ..., S_{A_n}\}$, can be transformed into n reasoning graphs of generated solutions $\{G_{A_1}, G_{A_2}, ..., G_{A_n}\}$.

Regarding the node features in the graph, we select the score from the *Base Verifier* and the node degree. We believe the score from the *Base Verifier* encapsulates the semantic information of solutions, and the node degree contains information about the graph structure. The *Base Verifier* is trained independently from the whole framework. It is designed to judge whether a single reasoning path of one solution is correct, which is a binary text classification task. After training, it can be used to verify any single solution and assign a $score \in (0, 1)$ to evaluate the likelihood of the solution being correct, where $score = 0.99$ suggests a 99% probability of the solution being correct. We use the score from the *Base Verifier* to better incorporate solution semantic information because, according to our experiments, it is challenging to model semantic information while modeling reasoning logic information. The score of a step is the same as its solution score. Therefore, for one step node V, it has many scores $\{score^a, score^b, ..., score^c\}$ from different solutions. The feature of one node V_i in the graph is then concatenated by the selected feature, which can be represented as:

$$\mathbf{V} = [score_i^{mean}, score_i^{max}, score_i^{min}, score_i^{num}, in\_degree_i], \quad (5)$$

where $\mathbf{V} \in \mathbb{R}^5$, $score_i^{mean}$ is the mean of all scores of one step V_i, $score_i^{max}$ is the maximum score, $score_i^{min}$ is the minimum score, $score_i^{num}$ is the number of scores, and in_degree_i is the in-degree of the step node V_i.

Algorithm 1 Reasoning graph construction algorithm

Input: generated solutions S_{A_i} which have the same final answers

Output: a reasoning graph G_{A_i}

```
node_num ← 0
node2id ← dict()
edges ← list()
for each reason_path in S_{A_i} do
    for each step in reason_path do
        if step not in node2id.keys() then
            node2id[step] ← node_num
            node_num ← node_num + 1
        end if
    end for
end for
for each reason_path in S_{A_i} do
    for each step in reason_path do
        start_node ← node2id[last_step]
        end_node ← node2id[step]
        if (start_node, end_node) not in edges then
            edges.add((start_node, end_node))
        end if
        last_step ← step
    end for
end for
G_{A_i} ← graph(node2id, edges)
```

In this way, we can obtain multiple reasoning graphs to represent all generated solutions from LLMs for a single math word problem question.

3.4 Verifier Design

Our designed verifier `GraphReason`,is used to evaluate the answer of a generated solutions group, which is also represented as a reasoning graph. This verifier has two inputs: the graph and the sum of solution scores. We employ the Graph Isomorphism Network (GIN) (Xu et al., 2019) to perform node feature propagation, thereby encoding the information from the reasoning graphs we obtained. The node feature is propagated and aggregated as follows:

$$h_v^{(k)} = MLP^{(k)}((1+\varepsilon^{(k)}) \cdot h_v^{(k-1)} + \sum\nolimits_{u \in N(v)} h_u^{(k-1)}), \quad (6)$$

where $h_v^{(k)}$ represents the state of node v after the kth update. $MLP^{(k)}$ refers to a multi-layer perceptron in the kth layer. $N(v)$ denotes all the neighbors of node v and ε is a learnable parameter. Then, we perform a sum readout to obtain the representation of the reasoning graph:

$$h_G = \sum_{v \in G} h_v^{(k)}, \quad (7)$$

where $h_G \in \mathbb{R}^5$. We set k to 3, signifying the application of three layers of GIN. Concurrently, the sum of the scores of solutions with the same final answer, A_i, denoted as $score_{A_i}$, is represented as follows:

$$score_A = \sum_{i \in S_A} score_i. \quad (8)$$

Then a reasoning graph can then be represented as:

$$\mathbf{G} = [h_G, score_A], \quad (9)$$

where $\mathbf{G} \in \mathbb{R}^6$.

The target label of the graph $\mathbf{y} \in \{0,1\}$ indicates whether the final answer matches the correct final answer. We compute the loss and train the verifier model by:

$$\mathcal{L} = \sum_{i=1}^{n} \mathcal{L}_{BCE}(label_i, f(\mathbf{G}_i)), \quad (10)$$

where i represents the number of solution subset among all n subsets after grouping solutions. The corresponding reasoning graph for this subset is denoted by $\mathbf{G}_i$, and $f()$ is a linear classifier.

3.5 Answer Verification

During the prediction stage, all generated solutions are processed in the same way as in the training stage. The trained verifier is then used to evaluate the scores of each reasoning graph, each of which represents a group of solutions that yield the same final answer. The final answer associated with the highest score is selected as our final predicted answer:

$$\hat{\mathbf{y}} = \mathbf{Answer}[\arg\max_i score_i], \quad (11)$$

where $score_i$ denotes the score of the reasoning graph $\mathbf{G}_i$, as determined by our verifier. **Answer** represents the list of all candidate final answers. By predicting the number of the optimal reasoning graph, we can determine the final predicted result of the current reasoning task.

	GSM8K	SVAMP	ASDiv-a	StrategyQA
Fine-tuning SOTA	57^a	57.4^b	75.3^c	73.9^d
9–12 year olds	60	-	-	-
gpt-3.5-turbo:				
Greedy Decode	72.7	78.7	93.0	65.0
Self-Consistency (Voting)	82.3	82.9	95.6	66.0
Verifier	66.9	73.1	92.8	69.3
Voting Verifier	85.4	84.8	96.9	70.7
DIVERSE (Step-aware Voting Verifier)	85.0	85.1	96.8	66.9
Reasoning Graph Verifier (Ours)	**85.7**	**85.4**	**97.0**	**71.2**

Table 1: The comparison experiment results of GraphReason, other verifiers, and other baselines. We primarily compare GraphReason with other verifiers which are all based on the same generated solutions from *gpt-3.5-turbo*

4 Experiments

In this section, we conducted extensive experiments to demonstrate the performance of GraphReason, along with a more in-depth analysis. Universally, we reproduced all types of verifiers to report their results based on the same generated solutions. Our experiments are conducted in two settings: Arithmetic Reasoning and Commonsense Reasoning. We ensured a fair comparison by setting the same random seed, using the same hardware environment, and applying similar hyperparameters. We used accuracy as the metric to evaluate the ability of solving math word problems, which determines whether the final answer is correct or not.

4.1 Training Details

For LLMs sampling, we use *gpt-3.5-turbo* as our base LLMs and set the temperature t to 1. All verifiers use the same LLMs' output. Regarding verifier training, we fine-tune on *bert-base-uncased* (Devlin et al., 2019). We employ the AdamW optimizer (Loshchilov and Hutter, 2019) to optimize the model parameters during training. We apply differential learning rates, setting the learning rate of the final linear classifier to 4e-2, while the other graph neural network layers are set to 4e-3. The activation layer between them is ReLU (Agarap, 2019). The batch size in each training step is set to 2. The batch size is small because the verifier needs to verify multiple reasoning graphs for a single question.

To ensure a fair comparison between the Voting Verifier, Simple Verifier, and GraphReason, we use the same trained base verifier for all three approaches.

The details of the datasets and baselines are provided in Appendix A and Appendix B, respectively.

4.2 Main Results

We present the main results in Table 1. As can be seen from the table, GraphReason significantly enhances the original *gpt-3.5-turbo*'s reasoning abilities across all three datasets, for instance, improving accuracy by 13.0% (72.7% $\rightarrow$ 85.7%) on GSM8K. It is also evident that our method surpasses other verifier methods with the same output from LLMs and achieves the state-of-the-art on all three datasets.

Additionally, the Step-aware Voting Verifier improves upon the Voting Verifier by recognizing that not all steps in an incorrect reasoning path are equally erroneous, and some steps may still be useful for reasoning. We believe this hypothesis is overly simplistic and cannot describe complex logical relationships among steps. According to Table 1, it leads to some metric decline, and the same finding also observed in the original paper. Furthermore, it does not perform well in the StrategyQA task, because there are no gold reasoning paths for the training of this commonsense reasoning task. In this task, the reasoning paths are generated and pseudo, indicating a requirement for gold labels at each step of the reasoning process. However, our paper consistently improves upon the Voting Verifier by considering complex relationship between different reasoning paths through reasoning graphs. We enhance the previous method, which did not consider relations in steps between different solutions, by 0.3% (85.4% $\rightarrow$ 85.7%), 0.3% (85.1% $\rightarrow$ 85.4%), 0.1% (96.9% $\rightarrow$ 97.0%), and 0.5% (70.7% $\rightarrow$ 71.2%) across the four datasets.

Moreover, GraphReason yields only a slight improvement in performance on ASDiv-a, and the results are nearly identical. One reason for this is that the math word problems from ASDiv-a are sim-

	GSM8K	▽	SVAMP	▽	ASDiv-a	▽
Reasoning Graph Verifier (Ours)	**85.7**	-	**85.4**	-	**97.0**	-
w/o solution semantic from base verifier	81.2	-4.5	83.1	-2.3	94.3	-2.7
w/o solution scores sum	82.8	-2.9	83.2	-2.2	95.6	-1.4
w/o reasoning graphs	85.4	-0.3	84.8	-0.6	96.9	-0.1

Table 2: The ablation experiment results of GraphReason. Missing each component leads to a decline in the final result.

pler compared to those in the other two datasets, based on our observations. In most cases, these problems do not require complex reasoning from a graph perspective to generate a satisfactory answer. It demonstrates that our method is particularly well-suited for such situations. We believe that GraphReason can offer more substantial improvements in the more complex scenario.

4.3 Ablation Study

We conducted an ablation study to evaluate the impact of each component on the overall performance of our method. Table 2 presents the results of this study, highlighting how these modules contribute to the improvement of the base model in distinct ways. It can be observed that the omission of any component leads to a decline in the final result. The solution semantics from the base verifier appear to be most crucial to GraphReason. The current method still relies on semantic information, which is reasonable since reasoning steps from different solutions require semantic information for better reasoning. We also notice that reasoning graphs bring a slight improvement to the entire method, thereby proving effectiveness of graph structure. The improvement is not substantial because we do not model the graph structure and semantic information simultaneously, and create a training gap here. Another essential factor is the complexity of graph classification, compounded by the presence of noise and limitations in our training data.

4.4 GraphReason with Different LLMs

To evaluate the compatibility of GraphReason and its effectiveness across various models, we additionally include *gpt-4* (OpenAI, 2023) and *PaLM-2* (Google, 2023) in our experiments. Given our limited computing resources, we utilize the same training data previously sampled from *gpt-3.5-turbo*. For testing in the GSM8K task, we select samples from 100 pieces of data from *gpt-4* and *PaLM-2* respectively. We conduct the sampling 10 times using three types of five exemplars, maintaining the same settings as in our previous experiments. Our method aims to enhance the original reasoning capabilities. Therefore, we do not include small-sized LMs, which typically exhibit weaker reasoning abilities.

	gpt-3.5-turbo	gpt-4	PaLM-2
Greedy Decode	72.7	87.0	53.0
Voting	82.3	94.0	71.0
Simple Verifier	66.9	89.0	36.0
Voting Verifier	85.4	**97.0**	77.0
DIVERSE	85.0	**97.0**	75.0
Ours	**85.7**	94.0	**78.0**

Table 3: The experimental results of GraphReason with different LLMs.

From Table 3, it is evident that our method enhances the original reasoning performance of both *GPT-4* and *PaLM-2*. However, there is a performance decline in *gpt-4* when compared with the best baselines. The performance of GraphReason is comparable to that of the voting method. We hypothesize that this is because the reasoning patterns of *GPT-4* differ from those of *GPT-3.5-Turbo*, and our verifier is trained specifically on *GPT-3.5-Turbo* samples in this setting.

5 Conclusion

In this paper, we propose GraphReason, a novel and general method to enhance the reasoning abilities of large language models. Our method is the first to approach reasoning logic of large language models from a graph perspective and verifies candidate reasoning paths accordingly. We demonstrate the superiority of GraphReason through extensive experiments.

Limitations

There are several limitations in the current research that contribute to performance that is not as good as expected:

- **Computing Resources**. Despite the impressive performance it achieves, our framework requires large language models like GPT3.5. Inference with these models is more time-consuming and costly than fine-tuning models like BERT(Devlin et al., 2019). Some experiments, such as hyper-parameter analysis, have already been conducted in related previous work and are not replicated here. Furthermore, due to limited computing resources, we have not conducted experiments with additional LLMs. We have chosen solely to use the representative LLM, GPT3.5, to compare the performance of the verifiers.
- **Labeled CoT data**. `GraphReason` is a complex verifier method that builds on graph classification, which requires more labeled data with well-annotated chain-of-thought reasoning paths for training. In the training of `GraphReason`, we use reasoning paths from LLMs' output which may introduce significant noise. If the training data included labeled reasoning graphs, the performance would improve significantly.
- **Other Reasoning Tasks**. There are many types of reasoning tasks beyond math word problems, such as Commonsense Reasoning (Talmor et al., 2019), Inductive Reasoning (Sinha et al., 2019), etc. Given that graph construction is a complex process, we have focused mainly on solving math word problems (Arithmetic Reasoning). This focus allows for a more convenient implementation of the merging of intermediate steps. In other cases, identifying similar steps can be challenging. On the other hand, a math word problem typically presents a greater variety of potential solutions.

Nevertheless, we believe that future studies, conducted by us or others, can overcome these limitations and further improve upon our approach.

References

Abien Fred Agarap. 2019. Deep learning using rectified linear units (relu). *Preprint*, arXiv:1803.08375.

Aakanksha Chowdhery, Sharan Narang, Jacob Devlin, Maarten Bosma, Gaurav Mishra, Adam Roberts, Paul Barham, Hyung Won Chung, Charles Sutton, Sebastian Gehrmann, Parker Schuh, Kensen Shi, Sasha Tsvyashchenko, Joshua Maynez, Abhishek Rao, Parker Barnes, Yi Tay, Noam Shazeer, Vinodkumar Prabhakaran, Emily Reif, Nan Du, Ben Hutchinson, Reiner Pope, James Bradbury, Jacob Austin, Michael Isard, Guy Gur-Ari, Pengcheng Yin, Toju Duke, Anselm Levskaya, Sanjay Ghemawat, Sunipa Dev, Henryk Michalewski, Xavier Garcia, Vedant Misra, Kevin Robinson, Liam Fedus, Denny Zhou, Daphne Ippolito, David Luan, Hyeontaek Lim, Barret Zoph, Alexander Spiridonov, Ryan Sepassi, David Dohan, Shivani Agrawal, Mark Omernick, Andrew M. Dai, Thanumalayan Sankaranarayana Pillai, Marie Pellat, Aitor Lewkowycz, Erica Moreira, Rewon Child, Oleksandr Polozov, Katherine Lee, Zongwei Zhou, Xuezhi Wang, Brennan Saeta, Mark Diaz, Orhan Firat, Michele Catasta, Jason Wei, Kathy Meier-Hellstern, Douglas Eck, Jeff Dean, Slav Petrov, and Noah Fiedel. 2022. Palm: Scaling language modeling with pathways. *Preprint*, arXiv:2204.02311.

Karl Cobbe, Vineet Kosaraju, Mohammad Bavarian, Mark Chen, Heewoo Jun, Lukasz Kaiser, Matthias Plappert, Jerry Tworek, Jacob Hilton, Reiichiro Nakano, Christopher Hesse, and John Schulman. 2021a. Training verifiers to solve math word problems. *arXiv preprint arXiv:2110.14168*.

Karl Cobbe, Vineet Kosaraju, Mohammad Bavarian, Mark Chen, Heewoo Jun, Lukasz Kaiser, Matthias Plappert, Jerry Tworek, Jacob Hilton, Reiichiro Nakano, Christopher Hesse, and John Schulman. 2021b. Training verifiers to solve math word problems. *Preprint*, arXiv:2110.14168.

Jacob Devlin, Ming-Wei Chang, Kenton Lee, and Kristina Toutanova. 2019. Bert: Pre-training of deep bidirectional transformers for language understanding. *Preprint*, arXiv:1810.04805.

Mor Geva, Daniel Khashabi, Elad Segal, Tushar Khot, Dan Roth, and Jonathan Berant. 2021. Did Aristotle Use a Laptop? A Question Answering Benchmark with Implicit Reasoning Strategies. *Transactions of the Association for Computational Linguistics (TACL)*.

Google. 2023. Palm 2 technical report. *Preprint*, arXiv:2305.10403.

Jie Huang and Kevin Chen-Chuan Chang. 2023. Towards reasoning in large language models: A survey. *Preprint*, arXiv:2212.10403.

Takeshi Kojima, Shixiang Shane Gu, Machel Reid, Yutaka Matsuo, and Yusuke Iwasawa. 2023. Large language models are zero-shot reasoners. *Preprint*, arXiv:2205.11916.

Andrew Lampinen, Ishita Dasgupta, Stephanie Chan, Kory Mathewson, Mh Tessler, Antonia Creswell, James McClelland, Jane Wang, and Felix Hill. 2022a. Can language models learn from explanations in context? In *Findings of the Association for Computational Linguistics: EMNLP 2022*, pages 537–563,

Abu Dhabi, United Arab Emirates. Association for Computational Linguistics.

Andrew K Lampinen, Ishita Dasgupta, Stephanie CY Chan, Kory Matthewson, Michael Henry Tessler, Antonia Creswell, James L McClelland, Jane X Wang, and Felix Hill. 2022b. Can language models learn from explanations in context? *arXiv preprint arXiv:2204.02329*.

Yifei Li, Zeqi Lin, Shizhuo Zhang, Qiang Fu, Bei Chen, Jian-Guang Lou, and Weizhu Chen. 2023. Making language models better reasoners with step-aware verifier. In *Proceedings of the 61st Annual Meeting of the Association for Computational Linguistics (Volume 1: Long Papers)*, pages 5315–5333, Toronto, Canada. Association for Computational Linguistics.

Zhongli Li, Wenxuan Zhang, Chao Yan, Qingyu Zhou, Chao Li, Hongzhi Liu, and Yunbo Cao. 2022. Seeking patterns, not just memorizing procedures: Contrastive learning for solving math word problems. In *Findings of the Association for Computational Linguistics: ACL 2022*, pages 2486–2496, Dublin, Ireland. Association for Computational Linguistics.

Ilya Loshchilov and Frank Hutter. 2019. Decoupled weight decay regularization. *Preprint*, arXiv:1711.05101.

Shen-yun Miao, Chao-Chun Liang, and Keh-Yih Su. 2020. A diverse corpus for evaluating and developing english math word problem solvers. In *Proceedings of the 58th Annual Meeting of the Association for Computational Linguistics*, pages 975–984.

OpenAI. 2023. Gpt-4 technical report. *Preprint*, arXiv:2303.08774.

Arkil Patel, Satwik Bhattamishra, and Navin Goyal. 2021. Are NLP models really able to solve simple math word problems? In *Proceedings of the 2021 Conference of the North American Chapter of the Association for Computational Linguistics: Human Language Technologies*, pages 2080–2094, Online. Association for Computational Linguistics.

Xinyu Pi, Qian Liu, Bei Chen, Morteza Ziyadi, Zeqi Lin, Qiang Fu, Yan Gao, Jian-Guang Lou, and Weizhu Chen. 2022. Reasoning like program executors. In *Proceedings of the 2022 Conference on Empirical Methods in Natural Language Processing*, pages 761–779, Abu Dhabi, United Arab Emirates. Association for Computational Linguistics.

Jack W. Rae, Sebastian Borgeaud, Trevor Cai, Katie Millican, Jordan Hoffmann, Francis Song, John Aslanides, Sarah Henderson, Roman Ring, Susannah Young, Eliza Rutherford, Tom Hennigan, Jacob Menick, Albin Cassirer, Richard Powell, George van den Driessche, Lisa Anne Hendricks, Maribeth Rauh, Po-Sen Huang, Amelia Glaese, Johannes Welbl, Sumanth Dathathri, Saffron Huang, Jonathan Uesato, John Mellor, Irina Higgins, Antonia Creswell, Nat McAleese, Amy Wu, Erich Elsen, Siddhant Jayakumar, Elena Buchatskaya, David Budden, Esme Sutherland, Karen Simonyan, Michela Paganini, Laurent Sifre, Lena Martens, Xiang Lorraine Li, Adhiguna Kuncoro, Aida Nematzadeh, Elena Gribovskaya, Domenic Donato, Angeliki Lazaridou, Arthur Mensch, Jean-Baptiste Lespiau, Maria Tsimpoukelli, Nikolai Grigorev, Doug Fritz, Thibault Sottiaux, Mantas Pajarskas, Toby Pohlen, Zhitao Gong, Daniel Toyama, Cyprien de Masson d'Autume, Yujia Li, Tayfun Terzi, Vladimir Mikulik, Igor Babuschkin, Aidan Clark, Diego de Las Casas, Aurelia Guy, Chris Jones, James Bradbury, Matthew Johnson, Blake Hechtman, Laura Weidinger, Iason Gabriel, William Isaac, Ed Lockhart, Simon Osindero, Laura Rimell, Chris Dyer, Oriol Vinyals, Kareem Ayoub, Jeff Stanway, Lorrayne Bennett, Demis Hassabis, Koray Kavukcuoglu, and Geoffrey Irving. 2022. Scaling language models: Methods, analysis & insights from training gopher. *Preprint*, arXiv:2112.11446.

Koustuv Sinha, Shagun Sodhani, Jin Dong, Joelle Pineau, and William L. Hamilton. 2019. CLUTRR: A diagnostic benchmark for inductive reasoning from text. In *Proceedings of the 2019 Conference on Empirical Methods in Natural Language Processing and the 9th International Joint Conference on Natural Language Processing (EMNLP-IJCNLP)*, pages 4506–4515, Hong Kong, China. Association for Computational Linguistics.

Alon Talmor, Jonathan Herzig, Nicholas Lourie, and Jonathan Berant. 2019. CommonsenseQA: A question answering challenge targeting commonsense knowledge. In *Proceedings of the 2019 Conference of the North American Chapter of the Association for Computational Linguistics: Human Language Technologies, Volume 1 (Long and Short Papers)*, pages 4149–4158, Minneapolis, Minnesota. Association for Computational Linguistics.

Karthik Valmeekam, Alberto Olmo, Sarath Sreedharan, and Subbarao Kambhampati. 2023. Large language models still can't plan (a benchmark for llms on planning and reasoning about change). *Preprint*, arXiv:2206.10498.

Siyuan Wang, Wanjun Zhong, Duyu Tang, Zhongyu Wei, Zhihao Fan, Daxin Jiang, Ming Zhou, and Nan Duan. 2022. Logic-driven context extension and data augmentation for logical reasoning of text. In *Findings of the Association for Computational Linguistics: ACL 2022*, pages 1619–1629, Dublin, Ireland. Association for Computational Linguistics.

Xuezhi Wang, Jason Wei, Dale Schuurmans, Quoc Le, Ed Chi, Sharan Narang, Aakanksha Chowdhery, and Denny Zhou. 2023. Self-consistency improves chain of thought reasoning in language models. *Preprint*, arXiv:2203.11171.

Jason Wei, Xuezhi Wang, Dale Schuurmans, Maarten Bosma, Ed Chi, Quoc Le, and Denny Zhou. 2022. Chain of thought prompting elicits reasoning in large language models. *arXiv preprint arXiv:2201.11903*.

Zhipeng Xie and Shichao Sun. 2019. A goal-driven tree-structured neural model for math word problems. In *Proceedings of the Twenty-Eighth International Joint Conference on Artificial Intelligence, IJCAI-19*, pages 5299–5305. International Joint Conferences on Artificial Intelligence Organization.

Keyulu Xu, Weihua Hu, Jure Leskovec, and Stefanie Jegelka. 2019. How powerful are graph neural networks? In *International Conference on Learning Representations*.

Ori Yoran, Alon Talmor, and Jonathan Berant. 2022. Turning tables: Generating examples from semi-structured tables for endowing language models with reasoning skills. In *Proceedings of the 60th Annual Meeting of the Association for Computational Linguistics (Volume 1: Long Papers)*, pages 6016–6031, Dublin, Ireland. Association for Computational Linguistics.

Dongxiang Zhang, Lei Wang, Luming Zhang, Bing Tian Dai, and Heng Tao Shen. 2019. The gap of semantic parsing: A survey on automatic math word problem solvers. *Preprint*, arXiv:1808.07290.

Jipeng Zhang, Lei Wang, Roy Ka-Wei Lee, Yi Bin, Yan Wang, Jie Shao, and Ee-Peng Lim. 2020. Graph-to-tree learning for solving math word problems. In *Proceedings of the 58th Annual Meeting of the Association for Computational Linguistics*, pages 3928–3937, Online. Association for Computational Linguistics.

Wayne Xin Zhao, Kun Zhou, Junyi Li, Tianyi Tang, Xiaolei Wang, Yupeng Hou, Yingqian Min, Beichen Zhang, Junjie Zhang, Zican Dong, Yifan Du, Chen Yang, Yushuo Chen, Zhipeng Chen, Jinhao Jiang, Ruiyang Ren, Yifan Li, Xinyu Tang, Zikang Liu, Peiyu Liu, Jian-Yun Nie, and Ji-Rong Wen. 2023. A survey of large language models. *Preprint*, arXiv:2303.18223.

Denny Zhou, Nathanael Schärli, Le Hou, Jason Wei, Nathan Scales, Xuezhi Wang, Dale Schuurmans, Claire Cui, Olivier Bousquet, Quoc Le, and Ed Chi. 2023. Least-to-most prompting enables complex reasoning in large language models. *Preprint*, arXiv:2205.10625.

A Datasets

We compared GraphReason with other methods on three different math word problem datasets: **GSM8K** (Cobbe et al., 2021a), **SVAMP** (Patel et al., 2021), and **ASDiv-a** (Miao et al., 2020) and one commonsense reasoning dataset: **StrategyQA** (Geva et al., 2021). We selected the subset ASDiv-a (arithmetic) from the original dataset ASDiv, which only involves arithmetic operations.

These three arithmetic reasoning datasets are more challenging than other math word problem datasets, making them more suitable for testing the reasoning capability of LLMs with a verifier. As the GSM8K dataset is the only one providing step-by-step solutions as chain-of-thought exemplars, we chose exemplars from the GSM8K training dataset and tested them on all three datasets. Additionally, the training data for the verifier also used the GSM8K training data. In this setting, we could also demonstrate the transfer learning and generalization ability of our method. The size of the training split from GSM8k is 1000. The test data sizes for GSM8K, SVAMP, and ASDiv-a are 1319, 1000, and 1218, respectively.

In the StrategyQA commonsense reasoning task, we set the number of exemplars to 8 and select pseudo-exemplars from (Li et al., 2023). Additionally, we conduct five sampling iterations for each context of LLMs. From the entire dataset, we select a subset of 1,000 instances, allocating 700 for training and 300 for testing.

B Baselines

In our evaluation, we consider the following baselines:

- **Greedy Decode** is a simple method that uses a greedy decoding strategy to sample once.
- **Self-Consistency (Voting)** (Wang et al., 2023) samples multiple times and selects the final answers based on majority voting.
- **Simple Verifier** (Cobbe et al., 2021b), which is also known as the Sampling and Re-ranking strategy, uses a verifier to assign scores to sampled solutions and selects the final answer with the highest score.
- **Voting Verifier** (Li et al., 2023) combines the Voting and Verifier approaches. It assigns total scores to answers from scores of all candidate solutions and selects the final answer with the highest score.
- **DIVERSE (Step-aware Voting Verifier)** (Li et al., 2023), which is the state-of-the-art method, considers the reasoning steps throughout the entire reasoning path. It recognizes that not all steps in an incorrect reasoning path are equally wrong and that some steps may still be useful for reasoning.

We primarily compare GraphReason with other verifiers using the same generated solutions from *gpt-3.5-turbo*. Additionally, we include some previous Fine-tuning state-of-the-art methods to reflect the strong reasoning ability of LLMs. The previous Fine-tuning SOTA methods are denoted as follows: a: (Cobbe et al., 2021b), b: (Pi et al., 2022), c: (Miao et al., 2020), d: (Chowdhery et al., 2022).

PROC2PDDL: Open-Domain Planning Representations from Texts

Tianyi Zhang[1*] **Li Zhang**[1*] **Zhaoyi Hou**[3]
Ziyu Wang[1] **Yuling Gu**[2] **Peter Clark**[2]
Chris Callison-Burch[1] **Niket Tandon**[2]
[1]University of Pennsylvania [2]Allen Institute for Artificial Intelligence
[3]University of Pittsburg
{zty|zharry|ccb}@upenn.edu

Abstract

Planning in a text-based environment continues to be a significant challenge for AI systems. Recent approaches have utilized language models to predict planning domain definitions (e.g., PDDL) but have only been evaluated in closed-domain simulated environments. To address this, we present PROC2PDDL, the first dataset containing open-domain procedural texts paired with expert-annotated PDDL representations. Using this dataset, we evaluate the task of predicting domain actions (parameters, preconditions, and effects). We experiment with various large language models (LLMs) and prompting mechanisms, including a novel instruction inspired by the zone of proximal development (ZPD), which reconstructs the task as incremental basic skills. Our results demonstrate that PROC2PDDL is highly challenging for end-to-end LLMs, with GPT-3.5's success rate close to 0% and GPT-4o's 38%. With ZPD instructions, GPT-4o's success rate increases to 45%, outperforming regular chain-of-thought prompting's 34%. Our analysis systematically examines both syntactic and semantic errors, providing insights into the strengths and weaknesses of language models in generating domain-specific programs.[1]

1 Introduction

Planning is the task of finding a sequence of actions to achieve a goal in a given environment (Fikes and Nilsson, 1971; LaValle, 2006). In real life, the environment is often described with natural language texts. To enable text-based, automated planning, recent work has used language models (LMs) to *generate plans* (Valmeekam et al., 2023a; Stein and Koller, 2023). However, this approach is found to fall short with regard to both performance and interpretability (Valmeekam et al., 2023c,b). Alternatively, another recent line of worked has instead used LMs to *translate* the natural language description of environments to planning domain definition language (PDDL) (Ghallab et al., 1998). This symbolic representation can then be solved by a planner in a plan (Collins et al., 2022; Lyu et al., 2023; Liu et al., 2023; Xie et al., 2023; Wong et al., 2023). Despite of the success of such a neurosymbolic method, all the above work has only been evaluated in **closed-domains** simulated environments such as a household (e.g., ALFRED (Shridhar et al., 2020)) or discrete object placement (e.g., BlocksWorld (Valmeekam et al., 2024)) (as shown in Table 1).

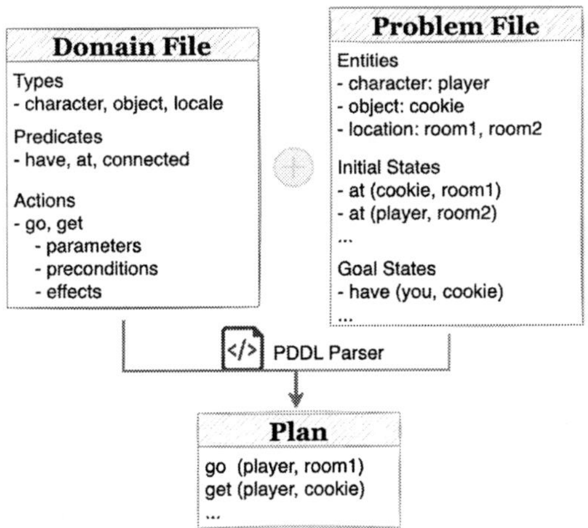

Figure 1: A PDDL solver produces a plan based on a minimal domain file and problem file. Previous work assumes the domain file as given, while we predict the action definitions in the domain file.

To enable **open-domain**, text-based planning, we propose PROC2PDDL, a dataset to evaluate models' ability to generate PDDL given procedural texts. PROC2PDDL consists of 27 pairs of open-domain procedures and PDDL representations. Each PDDL representation include a domain file $\mathbb{DF}$ that models the types, predicates, and actions, and a problem file $\mathbb{PF}$ that models the entities, initial states, and goal states, as illustrated in Figure 1. Because PROC2PDDL is not bound

*Equal contribution.
[1]Our resources can be found at https://github.com/zharry29/proc2pddl.

Proceedings of the 2nd Workshop on Natural Language Reasoning and Structured Explanations (@ACL 2024), pages 13–24
August 15, 2024

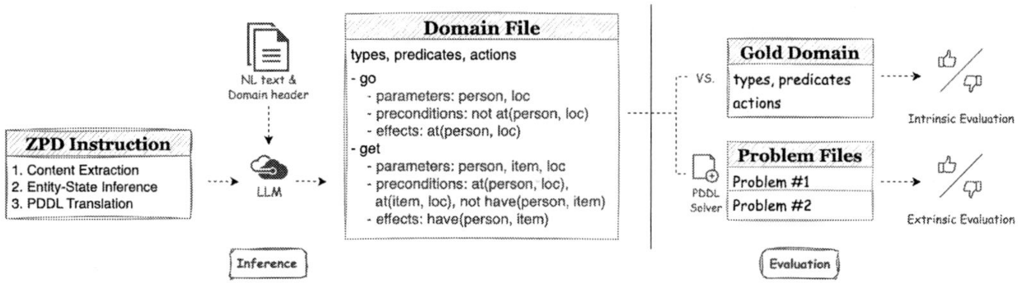

Figure 2: Our formulation of the 𝔻𝔽 action prediction task is as follows: given a natural language procedure text and a domain file header, a language model (LM) follows Zone of Proximal Development (ZPD) instructions in three sequential skills to predict domain actions, including parameters, preconditions, and effects. During evaluation, the predicted 𝔻𝔽 is compared to a gold reference and used to solve corresponding ℙ𝔽s.

to any simulation, the PDDL representations are manually annotated by experts trained on this task to ensure validity, resulting in 27 domain files and 95 problem files.

Using this dataset, we study the task of action modeling (Lindsay et al., 2017) formulated as follows. The input is some relevant natural language texts and the *header* of a 𝔻𝔽 (i.e., types, predicates, and names of actions). Based on a ZPD instruction, the output is the *domain actions* in the 𝔻𝔽 (i.e., parameters, preconditions, and effects). During evaluation, the predicted 𝔻𝔽 is 1) compared to a ground-truth 𝔻𝔽 as intrinsic evaluation, and 2) provided to a PDDL solver with ground-truth ℙ𝔽s for the existence and correctness of plans as extrinsic evaluation. Our system is delineated in Figure 2. In this formulation, our assumption of the 𝔻𝔽 header is necessary to ensure the consistency of semantics between the 𝔻𝔽 and the ℙ𝔽 for evaluation. It is also empirically motivated; for example, a kitchen robot may have access to the types like ‘ingredients’ and predicates like ‘diced’ via some information extraction system given descriptive texts, but it may still need to predict, for “swinging a knife”, the precondition that it is only safe to do so to the ‘ingredients’ and the effect that they will become ‘diced’.

Through our experiment, we show that the task of action modeling in Proc2PDDL is highly challenging to state-of-the-art LMs, where GPT-3.5 almost fails completely, GPT-4 can only generate exactly matching 𝔻𝔽s 16% of the time and solvable ℙ𝔽s 33% of the time, and GPT-4o demonstrate 18% 𝔻𝔽s accuracy and 37% ℙ𝔽s solving rate. By devising a ZPD instruction that prompt LMs to modularly generate PDDL through extraction-inference-translation approach, we improve action accuracy by 3% and problem solving by 2-7% . In our analysis, the syntactic errors indicate LMs’ weakness in generating low-resource and domain-specific programming languages (Cassano et al., 2023) like PDDL, while the semantic errors suggest LMs’ inaccuracies to reason about actions and environments.

	#𝔻𝔽	Datasets
Ours	27	Proc2PDDL
(Wong et al., 2023)	2	MineCraft, ALFRED
(Lyu et al., 2023)	1	SayCan
(Xie et al., 2023)	2	Blocksworld, ALFRED
(Liu et al., 2023)	7	Blocksworld, etc.
(Huang et al., 2023)	1	Tabletop
(Huang et al., 2022)	1	VirtualHome
(Silver et al., 2022)	18	Blocksworld, etc.
(Valmeekam et al., 2022)	2	Blocksworld, Logistics

Table 1: Our work proposes and evaluates models using Proc2PDDL which is open-domain and based on procedural texts, while past work has relied on closed-domain benchmarks which can be expressed with a singular 𝔻𝔽 with a fixed set of actions, based on some simulation.

2 Task Formulation

The task of predicting a planning domain definition in a text-based environment can be seen as translating natural language texts to PDDL symbolic language, which consists of a domain file (𝔻𝔽) and one or more problem files (ℙ𝔽s).

A 𝔻𝔽 defines all actions in the environment:

- parameters (e.g., water, pot) as a list of typed variables
- preconditions (e.g., water and pot belongs to player; water is not treated) as a conjunctive normal form of predicates
- effect (e.g., water is treated) as a conjunctive normal form of predicates

A ℙ𝔽 defines the initial and goal environments:

- initial states (e.g., bucket is empty)
- goal states (e.g., bucket is filled with rainwater; rainwater is treated)

We say that a $\mathbb{DF}$ and a $\mathbb{PF}$ can be solved if there exists a sequence of actions $A_1, \ldots, A_n$ that results in a transition from the initial state to the goal state.

Traditionally, the task of text-based PDDL generation involves predicting $\mathbb{PF}$ based on text $\mathbb{T}$, where a successfully generated $\mathbb{PF}$ can be solved by the predefined $\mathbb{DF}$.

In this paper, we address an alternative formulation, action modeling (A), in which the generated $\mathbb{DF}$, given text $\mathbb{T}$ and the domain header H[2], is capable of producing plans for $\mathbb{PF}$s.

3 Dataset

We introduce the PROC2PDDL dataset of 27 different $\mathbb{T}$-$\mathbb{DF}$-$\mathbb{PF}$s tuples, drawing procedural texts from wikiHow articles of various topics (see Appendix A). A class of graduate students in a U.S. university with prior knowledge of PDDL are each given a wikiHow article and annotate a $\mathbb{DF}$ and multiple corresponding $\mathbb{PF}$s from the article, each with a gold plan to solve it. On average, there are 13.33 defined actions in a $\mathbb{DF}$ and 8.07 instantiated actions in a gold plan. In this work, all our data is used for evaluation, as all our methods are without task specific model training. Some sample data of PROC2PDDL can be found in Appendix B.

4 Methodology

We first introduce a novel prompt design option, ZPD, and then discuss the choices of text format ($\mathbb{T}$), which can range from 10 to 2,000 tokens and influence the selection of LMs.

4.1 ZPD Prompt Design

To predict domain actions A based on relevant $\mathbb{T}$ and the header H, we prompt an LM in zero-shot or few-shot instructions. Our instruction employs Zone of Proximal Development (ZPD) theory proposed for human learning (Vygotsky and Cole, 1978), which is a variant of the chain-of-thought (CoT) approach. In typical CoT, a task is decomposed into several constituents (steps), i.e., parameters, precondition, and effect. In contrast, according to ZPD, the complex PROC2PDDL task is decomposed into atomic **skills**: 1) *extracting* the relevant *description* of an action; 2) *extracting* and *inferring* the incorporated *entities* and their *state changes*; and 3) *translating* the entity-state changes to accessible PDDL predicates. Next, we establish the relationships between these atomic skills: to perform the task, each skill is a prerequisite for the next. Finally, we explicitly instruct the LMs to incrementally perform the three basic skills, leading to the successful completion of the PROC2PDDL task (the prompt can be found in Appendix D):

1. Extraction: describe each action, including the expected preconditions and effects;
2. Inference: list the involved entities and their state changes;
3. Translation: based on the information above, convert $\mathbb{T}$ to PDDL.

[2] The domain header includes types, predicates, and names of actions in $\mathbb{DF}$. As the information specified by H is guaranteed to be consistent with that of the $\mathbb{PF}$s, the evaluation is well-defined.

Model %	Intrinsic action acc.	Extrinsic $\mathbb{PF}$ solve
gpt-3.5	0.2	1.0
gpt-4	15.9	33.7
+ CoT	9.3	21.1
+ ZPD	**18.1**	**35.8**
+ ZPD, 3 shot	11.9	23.2
gpt-4o	18.2	37.9
+ CoT	19.5	33.7
+ ZPD	**21.4**	**45.3**
+ ZPD, 3 shot	20.3	40.0
gold	100	100

Table 2: The intrinsic and extrinsic evaluation results for all main models. gpt-4(o) demonstrates non-trivial performance. With a ZPD instruction, the performance improves consistently.

Model %	Parameter	Precondition	Effect
gpt-4	36.7	31.1	**53.0**
+ CoT	29.7	25	54.7
+ ZPD	**42.2**	29.7	48.1
gpt-4o	45.1	31.1	**62.5**
+ CoT	52.4	34.2	54.1
+ ZPD	**53.5**	**40.1**	53.5

Table 3: The generation accuracy of each component in actions has been evaluated. The ZPD instruction clearly aids in identifying implicit parameters (entities). Predicting preconditions is more challenging than predicting effects, as it requires a greater depth of implicit knowledge of entity states.

4.2 Choice of Input Text

We also consider the following choices of wikiHow text as $\mathbb{T}$.

Prompt without text (w/o $\mathbb{T}$) is an ablation baseline where the model predicts A solely based on H. Naturally, none of the three aforementioned stages are involved in this prompt condition.

Model %	Intrinsic action acc.	Extrinsic $\mathbb{PF}$ solve
w/o $\mathbb{T}$ (baseline)	13.7	26.3
$\mathbb{T}$ =sum	15.9	33.7
$\mathbb{T}$ =sum, ZPD	**18.1**	**35.8**
$\mathbb{T}$ =map	11.8	13.7
$\mathbb{T}$ =map, ZPD	8.9	26.3
$\mathbb{T}$ =rel	11.6	27.4
$\mathbb{T}$ =rel, ZPD	12.2	21.1
$\mathbb{T}$ =all	12.1	28.4
$\mathbb{T}$ =all, ZPD	12.1	31.6

Table 4: Performance of GPT-4 using different portions of text $\mathbb{T}$. Metrics include action-wide accuracy and the proportion of $\mathbb{PF}$s that can be solved.

Prompt with text (w/ $\mathbb{T}$) additionally provides the model with four different portions of $\mathbb{T}$, involving the three aforementioned stages, as follows:
($\mathbb{T}$ = all): All steps in a wikiHow article.
($\mathbb{T}$ = rel): In PROC2PDDL, each wikiHow article consists of step paragraphs that may or may not be used in defining the actions in the $\mathbb{DF}$. Hence, a mapping between actions and steps is also annotated. This context includes relevant steps to all actions in a $\mathbb{DF}$. (e.g., Step 1. Find fresh water... Step 2. Collect food... Step 7. Set up camp...)
($\mathbb{T}$ = map): Each action is mapped with steps based on the annotated mapping in PROC2PDDL.
(e.g., clean_water: Step 1. Find fresh water...)
($\mathbb{T}$ = sum): An one-line summary of each action annotated in PROC2PDDL.
(e.g., clean_water; boil water to clean it)
The four prompts are increasingly general. Distinguishing from the required skills, the full text condition demands accurate information extraction, while the text summary clearly defines the action but requires the model's robust ability to infer implicit entity states. All prompts request an exact translation.

4.3 Experiments

We conducted experiments with three large language models[3]: GPT-3.5-turbo-16k, GPT-4-32k (dated June 2023), and GPT-4o. For GPT-4-32k, we used a maximum token limit of 10,000. GPT-3.5-turbo-16k and GPT-4o were tested with theirs default hyperparameters. The few-shot examples can be found in Appendix C.

[3]Due to the need for very long input and output, the choice of open-source models is limited. We are in progress of implementing `Mixtral-8x7B`.

5 Evaluation and Analysis

Now that a model generates the parameters, preconditions, and effects for each action, we have a complete $\mathbb{DF}$. We evaluate it in two ways (Figure 2). *Intrinsically*, we semantically compare the predicted A with the ground-truth provided by our PROC2PDDL and report an action-wide accuracy. Equivalence of two action definitions does not depend on the naming of variables nor on the order within conjunctions (detailed in Appendix E). *Extrinsically*, to measure actions' coherence, a BFS-based PDDL solver[4] attempts to solve ground-truth $\mathbb{PF}$s with the predicted $\mathbb{DF}$ and a success rate is reported. An unsolved $\mathbb{PF}$ is caused by (1.) no plan can be found, or (2.) the solver runs for more than 30 seconds, or (3.) the solver returns an error (usually a syntax error in the generated PDDL).

The intrinsic and extrinsic results are shown in Table 2. `gpt-3.5-turbo` which achieves impressive performance on many tasks has a close-to-zero performance. In contrast, `gpt-4` performs significantly better with 18% action prediction accuracy and 36% solve rate of $\mathbb{PF}$s. The most advanced `gpt-4o` presents the highest performance, with 21% action accuracy and 45% $\mathbb{PF}$s solving rate. Still, the performance is far worse than ideal, showing that even a simplified open-domain planning formulation is challenging to state-of-the-art LMs.

ZPD Instruction Analysis

ZPD is helpful in each setting since it explicitly spells out many implicit entities and state changes in the inference stage which are critical to predicting parameters. In most situations, the model summarizes the action and extracts the entity states correctly, though sometimes missing a few implicit entities. However, ZPD's bottleneck lies in the translation stage, during which there are mainly three types of errors.

1. mismatched predicates: the model uses `(at ?loc ?item)` instead of `(inventory ?item)`;
2. hallucinated predicates: the model creates a new predicate `(soaked ?item)` while neglecting the existing `(submerged ?item)`;
3. complicated predicates: the model adds unnecessary predicates `(inventory ?submerged_item - item)` when already has `(inventory ?item)`.

[4]`https://github.com/pucrs-automated-planning/pddl-parser`

	Unsolved			Solved	
	Syntactic Error	Bad Action	Good Action	Bad Plan	Good Plan
gpt-4	3	7	2	0	3

Table 5: A small-sample inspection shows that models make both syntactic and semantic errors.

To address these, we leave to future work to demonstrate and standardize the translation process by clearly describing all necessary entity-state change and encouraging the model to compare and strictly match the given predicates. Finer-grained evaluation results are shown in Table 3 to tease out the performance regarding such component within an action. It is clear that the LM is worse at predicting preconditions than at predicting effects. This is understandable as procedural texts like wikiHow tend to be less explicit about predictions than about effects (e.g., from 'bake for 10 minutes' it is obvious that the food will be baked, but it is unclear what state it had been in).

Text Format Analysis

As shown in Table 4, in w/o $\mathbb{T}$ setting, fully relying on its implicit knowledge, the model is already capable of inferring PDDL syntactically and semantically. In w/ $\mathbb{T}$ settings, our model shows an 'U' performance in terms of the text length. Using a sentence-long description for each action ($\mathbb{T}$ = `sum`) provided by PROC2PDDL, the model achieves the best performance among all, showing a strong deduction ability with the limited but precise NL input. The $\mathbb{T}$ = `all` setting ensues, which requires the most extraction rather than inference. In contrast, the middle ones ($\mathbb{T}$ = `rel/map`) with decreasing signal-to-noise ratio lead to worse results, indicating its shortage of extraction-inference trade-off. The signals contain both the described entity states and step relations, explicitly and implicitly. This shortage may come less from the entity states *(e.g., fish, spear in hunt_fish)*, but more from the relation between actions *(e.g., make_spear to hunt_fish)* which may be expressed in the $\mathbb{T}$ = `sum` and `all` settings.

Case Analysis

To provide deeper insights into model performance, we manually inspect the model output of `gpt-4` on all 6 examples (15 $\mathbb{PF}$s) in the development set. We consider the following scenarios.

Unsolved Whenever the predicted $\mathbb{DF}$ cannot solve a $\mathbb{PF}$, either a syntactic or a semantic error has occurred. For a **syntactic error**, the output may contain illegal expressions that cannot be parsed. For example, `(inventory ?player (clean ?strips))` is unacceptable because the arguments to a predicate must be atomic types, not another predicate. For a **semantic error** (namely, a 'bad action'), we identify the first problematic action that differs with the ground-truth. For example, if the action `cut_plant` misses a critical effect of `(inventory ?player ?stalk)`, then other actions such as `graft_stalk` requiring it cannot be executed. At times, there could be false negatives where the predicted action definitions are in fact reasonable but still cannot lead to a solution (namely, a 'good action').

Solved Even when the predicted $\mathbb{DF}$ solves a $\mathbb{PF}$, the plan may be different from the gold plan. It is naturally possible that the predicted plan is a fluke made possible by under-specified preconditions or over-exaggerated effects, as well as loopholes in the $\mathbb{PF}$ leading to unreasonable shortcuts. For the example in Figure 1, a model could *cheat* by defining the action `get` by not requiring the person and object to be in the same location; thus, the predicted plan would unreasonably omit the action go. However, at times, the predicted plan could also be a reasonable alternative.

The statistics of these errors are shown in Table 5. When no solution can be found, true negative is highly likely as the model indeed makes aforementioned mistakes during action prediction. When some solution is found, false positive is still possible as the predicted plan may be unreasonable. See attached materials for a complete error analysis of these examples. Our aforementioned future pipeline that separates summarization and translation would likely mitigate these errors.

6 Conclusion

We present PROC2PDDL, the first open-domain dataset that juxtaposes natural language and planning domain definition language. Our experiments show that ZPD instructions facilitate LMs' performance, while still find it challenging to translate the precondition and effects of actions. We hope our instruction design, evaluations and dataset help future progress towards integrating the best of LM and formal planning.

7 Limitations

Any planning language, including PDDL which we consider in this work, is an approximation of planning in the real world and cannot accurately reflect its complexity. Due to the consideration for simplicity in the annotation process, we use the primitive version of PDDLs, with restricted expressions and syntax, instead of newer versions of the planning language which extend its syntax in a variety of way.

Annotating PROC2PDDL is extremely costly as it requires knowledge of PDDL and much effort to translate procedural texts to PDDL. Thus, our dataset is relatively small with a limited range of topics. Due to the highly complex and subjective nature of the annotation process, each annotated example may reflect idiosyncratic though processes and biases of the individual annotator.

As with many similar works, there is a known gap between high-level planning such as ours (with high-level actions like "boil") and the actions used by present-day robots (with low-level motor functions like "move"). However, like similar works, we believe our efforts can see more practical application in the near future.

Our modeling efforts so far have mainly considered options of zero-shot prompting. There of course exists many other approaches including the few-shot setting, fine-tuning, and the model distillaion paradigm, which we plan to experiment with in the future. Moreover, our evaluation is imperfect in that even a well-annotated DF-PF pair might have multiple successful plans. Manual inspection is still necessary to accurately gauge models.

Acknowledgements

This research is supported in part by the Office of the Director of National Intelligence (ODNI), Intelligence Advanced Research Projects Activity (IARPA), via the HIATUS Program contract #2022-22072200005. The views and conclusions contained herein are those of the authors and should not be interpreted as necessarily representing the official policies, either expressed or implied, of ODNI, IARPA, or the U.S. Government. The U.S. Government is authorized to reproduce and distribute reprints for governmental purposes notwithstanding any copyright annotation therein.

References

Federico Cassano, John Gouwar, Francesca Lucchetti, Claire Schlesinger, Carolyn Jane Anderson, Michael Greenberg, Abhinav Jangda, and Arjun Guha. 2023. Knowledge transfer from high-resource to low-resource programming languages for code llms. arXiv preprint arXiv:2308.09895.

Katherine M. Collins, Catherine Wong, Jiahai Feng, Megan Wei, and Joshua B. Tenenbaum. 2022. Structured, flexible, and robust: benchmarking and improving large language models towards more human-like behavior in out-of-distribution reasoning tasks.

Richard E Fikes and Nils J Nilsson. 1971. Strips: A new approach to the application of theorem proving to problem solving. Artificial intelligence, 2(3-4):189–208.

Malik Ghallab, Adele Howe, Craig Knoblock, Drew McDermott, Ashwin Ram, Manuela Veloso, Daniel Weld, and David Wilkins. 1998. PDDL - the planning domain definition language. Technical Report "CVC TR-98-003/DSC TR-1165", Yale Center for Computational Vision and Control.

Wenlong Huang, Pieter Abbeel, Deepak Pathak, and Igor Mordatch. 2022. Language models as zero-shot planners: Extracting actionable knowledge for embodied agents. In International Conference on Machine Learning, pages 9118–9147. PMLR.

Wenlong Huang, Fei Xia, Dhruv Shah, Danny Driess, Andy Zeng, Yao Lu, Pete Florence, Igor Mordatch, Sergey Levine, Karol Hausman, et al. 2023. Grounded decoding: Guiding text generation with grounded models for robot control. arXiv preprint arXiv:2303.00855.

Steven M LaValle. 2006. Planning algorithms. Cambridge university press.

Alan Lindsay, Jonathon Read, Joao Ferreira, Thomas Hayton, Julie Porteous, and Peter Gregory. 2017. Framer: Planning models from natural language action descriptions. In Proceedings of the International Conference on Automated Planning and Scheduling, volume 27, pages 434–442.

Bo Liu, Yuqian Jiang, Xiaohan Zhang, Qiang Liu, Shiqi Zhang, Joydeep Biswas, and Peter Stone. 2023. Llm+p: Empowering large language models with optimal planning proficiency.

Qing Lyu, Shreya Havaldar, Adam Stein, Li Zhang, Delip Rao, Eric Wong, Marianna Apidianaki, and Chris Callison-Burch. 2023. Faithful chain-of-thought reasoning.

Mohit Shridhar, Jesse Thomason, Daniel Gordon, Yonatan Bisk, Winson Han, Roozbeh Mottaghi, Luke Zettlemoyer, and Dieter Fox. 2020. Alfred: A benchmark for interpreting grounded instructions for everyday tasks. In Proceedings of the IEEE/CVF conference on computer vision and pattern recognition, pages 10740–10749.

Tom Silver, Varun Hariprasad, Reece S Shuttleworth, Nishanth Kumar, Tomás Lozano-Pérez, and Leslie Pack Kaelbling. 2022. Pddl planning with pretrained large language models. In NeurIPS 2022 Foundation Models for Decision Making Workshop.

Katharina Stein and Alexander Koller. 2023. Autoplanbench:: Automatically generating benchmarks for llm planners from pddl. arXiv preprint arXiv:2311.09830.

Karthik Valmeekam, Matthew Marquez, Alberto Olmo, Sarath Sreedharan, and Subbarao Kambhampati. 2023a. Planbench: An extensible benchmark for evaluating large language models on planning and reasoning about change. In Thirty-seventh Conference on Neural Information Processing Systems Datasets and Benchmarks Track.

Karthik Valmeekam, Matthew Marquez, Alberto Olmo, Sarath Sreedharan, and Subbarao Kambhampati. 2024. Planbench: An extensible benchmark for evaluating large language models on planning and reasoning about change. Advances in Neural Information Processing Systems, 36.

Karthik Valmeekam, Matthew Marquez, Sarath Sreedharan, and Subbarao Kambhampati. 2023b. On the planning abilities of large language models–a critical investigation. arXiv preprint arXiv:2305.15771.

Karthik Valmeekam, Alberto Olmo, Sarath Sreedharan, and Subbarao Kambhampati. 2022. Large language models still can't plan (a benchmark for llms on planning and reasoning about change). arXiv preprint arXiv:2206.10498.

Karthik Valmeekam, Alberto Olmo, Sarath Sreedharan, and Subbarao Kambhampati. 2023c. Large language models still can't plan (a benchmark for llms on planning and reasoning about change).

Lev Semenovich Vygotsky and Michael Cole. 1978. Mind in society: Development of higher psychological processes. Harvard university press.

Lionel Wong, Jiayuan Mao, Pratyusha Sharma, Zachary S Siegel, Jiahai Feng, Noa Korneev, Joshua B Tenenbaum, and Jacob Andreas. 2023. Learning adaptive planning representations with natural language guidance. arXiv preprint arXiv:2312.08566.

Yaqi Xie, Chen Yu, Tongyao Zhu, Jinbin Bai, Ze Gong, and Harold Soh. 2023. Translating natural language to planning goals with large-language models.

A Topics

Below are a list of the titles of wikiHow articles in PROC2PDDL, chosen per the requirement of a gruaduate-level university class.

- create secret society
- throw an anime party
- open a coconut
- calculate pi
- hack
- get out of quicksand
- make a detective kit
- lock picking
- make papyrus
- survive on a desert island
- survive in the jungle
- survive a war
- survive a comet hitting earth
- survive a nuclear attack
- survive in the woods
- survive deserted island
- survive shark attack
- survive emp attack

Each topic may have one or more annotated $\mathbb{DF}$s representing different domains. The homogeneity of the last 7 topics is due to the class' topic of interactive fictions.

B Sample Data: $\mathbb{T}$, $\mathbb{DF}$, and $\mathbb{PF}$

To exemplify PROC2PDDL, below is an example procedural text $\mathbb{T}$ titled 'survive in the jungle', up to the third step, truncating the rest.

```
1. Collect rainfall from leaves and bamboo
   stalks. Look for large leaves that collect
   rainfall and bend them into a funnel to pour
   the water into a bottle or straight into
   your mouth. Bend bamboo stalks to let the
   water that collects in the compartments flow
   out into a container or break the bamboo
   compartment off at the line that goes across
   the stalk to use it as a water bottle. You
   could also look for rock formations that
   form natural pools and collect rainwater,
   but it is best to do this after a fresh
   rainfall to avoid pools that have been
   sitting for a long time and may be
   contaminated with bacteria. If you don't
   have a water bottle or other container to
   collect water, try to find other natural
   containers in the jungle such as a coconut
   shell or piece of wood shaped like a bowl.
   You can also leave these items out when it
   rains to collect the fresh water.

2. Boil water from streams to kill any bacteria.
   Look for running streams to find fresh
   water. Filter out any particles through a
   sock, shirt, or other fabric, then start a
   fire and boil the water to kill bacteria
   that can make you sick. If you don't have a
   pot to boil water in, then you can use a tin
   can, single-walled stainless steel water
   bottle, or any other metal container. If you
   have no way of making a fire or boiling the
   water, then you should avoid drinking water
   from streams. It can be contaminated with
   many types of bacteria from animals that
   will make you very sick. Always avoid
```

drinking water from stagnant pools as the water is likely contaminated.

3. Make a solar water still with a container and a plastic sheet. Dig a hole in an area that receives at least some direct sunlight and put a container, such as a water bottle or can, in the middle of the hole. Fill the space between the sides of the hole and the container with wet leaves. Place a plastic sheet over the top of the hole and put rocks or other heavy objects around the edges to hold it in place. Put a small stone in the middle of the sheet above the container. The plastic sheet will accumulate condensation that will drip down the underside of the sheet and into the container. This water is distilled and safe to drink. You can use natural containers such as bamboo or a coconut shell if you don't have a bottle or can. A solar still does not collect large amounts of water. It should be used as a supplemental source of water rather than a primary source.

......

Below is a sample annotated $\mathbb{DF}$ of the above:

```
(define (domain survive_in_the_jungle)
   (:requirements :strips :typing)
   (:types
       stone wood bamboo_container water fire
            sos_sign fruit - item
       basecamp - location
       ill dehydrated hungry - condition
       player
       direction
   )

   (:predicates
      (has_bamboo ?loc - location) ; this
           location has bamboo to create a
           container
      (has_rainfall ?loc - location) ; this
           location has received rainfall to
           collect water
      (has_fruit ?loc - location) ; this location
            has fruits to pick
      (treated ?water - water) ; True if the
           water has been decontaimated by
           boiling it
      (is ?c - condition ?p - player) ; True if
           the player is under the specified
           condition
      (at ?obj - object ?loc - location) ; an
           object is at a location
      (inventory ?player ?item) ; an item is in
           the player's inventory
      (connected ?loc1 - location ?dir -
           direction ?loc2 - location) ; location
            1 is connected to location 2 in the
           direction
      (blocked ?loc1 - location ?dir - direction
           ?loc2 - location) ; the connection
           between location 1 and 2 in currently
           blocked
   )

   (:action go ; navigate to an adjacent
        location
      :parameters (?dir - direction ?p - player ?
          l1 - location ?l2 - location)
      :precondition (and (at ?p ?l1) (connected ?
          l1 ?dir ?l2) (not (blocked ?l1 ?dir ?
          l2)))
      :effect (and (at ?p ?l2) (not (at ?p ?l1)))
   )

   (:action get ; pick up an item and put it in
        the inventory
      :parameters (?item - item ?p - player ?l1 -
           location)
      :precondition (and (at ?p ?l1) (at ?item ?
          l1))
      :effect (and (inventory ?p ?item) (not (at
          ?item ?l1)))
   )

   (:action get_bamboo_container; get a bamboo
        container using surrounding bamboo
      :parameters (?p - player ?loc - location)
      :precondition (and (at ?p ?loc) (has_bamboo
           ?loc))
      :effect (inventory ?p bamboo_container)
   )

   (:action collect_rain_water
      :parameters (?p - player ?loc - location)
      :precondition (and (at ?p ?loc) (inventory
          ?p bamboo_container) (has_rainfall ?
          loc))
      :effect (and (inventory ?p water) (not (
          treated water)))
   )

   (:action create_fire
      :parameters (?p - player ?loc - location)
      :precondition (and (at ?p ?loc) (inventory
          ?p stone) (inventory ?p wood))
      :effect (and (at fire ?loc) (not (inventory
           ?p stone)) (not (inventory ?p wood)))
   )

   (:action treat_water
      :parameters (?p - player ?loc - location)
      :precondition (and (inventory ?p water) (
          not (treated water)) (at fire ?loc))
      :effect (and (treated water))
   )

   (:action drink_water
      :parameters (?p - player)
      :precondition (and (inventory ?p water) (
          treated water))
      :effect (not (is dehydrated ?p))
   )

   (:action drink_untreated_water
      :parameters (?p - player)
      :precondition (and (inventory ?p water) (
          not (treated water)))
      :effect (is ill ?p)
   )

   (:action create_sos_sign
      :parameters (?p - player)
      :precondition (and (inventory ?p stone) (at
           ?p basecamp))
      :effect (and (not (inventory ?p stone)) (at
           sos_sign basecamp))
```

```
    )

    (:action pick_fruit
      :parameters (?p - player ?loc - location)
      :precondition (and (at ?p ?loc) (has_fruit
          ?loc))
      :effect (inventory ?p fruit)
    )

    (:action eat_fruit
      :parameters (?p - player)
      :precondition (and (is hungry ?p) (
          inventory ?p fruit))
      :effect (and (not (inventory ?p fruit)) (
          not (is hungry ?p)))
    )

    (:action escape
      :parameters (?p - player)
      :precondition (and (at ?p basecamp) (at
          sos_sign basecamp) (not (is hungry ?p))
           (not (is dehydrated ?p)) (not (is ill
           ?p)))
      :effect (not (at ?p basecamp))
    )
)
```

Below is an annotated $\mathbb{PF}$ of the above:

```
(define (problem escape)
    (:domain survive_in_the_jungle)

    (:objects
      npc - player
      jungle bamboo_forrest basecamp - location
      in out north south east west up down -
          direction
      stone wood sos_sign - item
      ill dehydrated hungry - condition
    )

    (:init
      (at npc basecamp)
      (connected basecamp west bamboo_forrest)
      (connected bamboo_forrest east basecamp)
      (connected basecamp east jungle)
      (connected jungle west basecamp)

      (has_bamboo bamboo_forrest)
      (has_fruit jungle)
      (has_rainfall jungle)

      (at stone bamboo_forrest)
      (at stone basecamp)
      (at wood jungle)

      (is dehydrated npc)
      (is hungry npc)
    )

    (:goal (and (not (at npc basecamp)) (not (at
        npc bamboo_forrest)) (not (at npc jungle)
        ) ))
)
```

C Few-shot Examples

```
Example 1:
action: slide_straw_over_skewer

text: Slide a segment of plastic straw over the
    2 skewers. Cut a segment of a plastic straw
    that is equal to the width between the wheel
     wells on your car. Then, slide it onto 1 of
     the skewers that's attached to a wheel. Do
    the same with the other skewer.

 pddl_action:
 (:action slide_straw_over_skewer
 :parameters (?straw1 - straw ?straw2 - straw ?
     skewer1 - skewer ?skewer2 - skewer ?wheel1
     - wheel ?wheel2 - wheel)
 :precondition (and
 (attached ?skewer1 ?wheel1)
 (attached ?skewer2 ?wheel2)
 (equal_width ?straw1 ?skewer1)
 (equal_width ?straw2 ?skewer2))
 :effect (and
 (over ?straw1 ?skewer1)
 (over ?straw2 ?skewer2)))

entity_state_inference:
- action name: slide_straw_over_skewer
- summarize action: The action involves cutting
    a segment of a plastic straw and sliding it
    over two skewers attached to wheels. The
    straw segments should be equal to the width
    between the wheel wells on a car.
- what is needed to do the action: A segment of
    a plastic straw, two skewers attached to
    wheels.

- what is the result: The straw segments are
    slid over the skewers, which helps in
    maintaining the structure of the car and
    providing stability to the wheels.

- entities:
 - entity name: plastic straw segment
 - before: Not cut and not on skewers
 - after: Cut and slid onto skewers
 - entity name: skewer
 - before: Without straw segments
 - after: With straw segments slid onto them
 - entity name: wheel
 - before: Attached to skewers, without straw
     segments on the skewers
 - after: Attached to skewers, with straw
     segments on the skewers

Example 2:
action: mix_sand_with_color

text: Close the bags tightly, then shake and
    squeeze them to mix the sand. Zip the bags
    shut tightly first. Next, shake the bags to
    help distribute the food coloring. You can
    also gently squeeze and massage the sand
    through the bags. Keep doing this until the
    color is even. Add more food coloring if the
     color is too light for you. Keep in mind
    that the sand will dry lighter.

pddl_action:
(:action mix_sand_with_color
:parameters (?bag - bag ?sand - sand ?color -
    food_coloring)
:precondition (and (sealed ?bag) (contains ?bag
    ?sand) (contains ?bag ?color) (not (
```

```
    evenly_colored ?sand)))
:effect (evenly_colored ?sand))''',

entity_state_inference:
- action name: mix_sand_with_color
- summarize action: This action involves mixing
    colored sand by sealing bags containing sand
     and food coloring, then shaking, squeezing,
     and massaging the bags until the sand color
     is evenly distributed. More food coloring
    may be added if the color is too light, with
     the understanding that the sand will dry
    lighter.
- what is needed to do the action: Sealed bags
    containing sand and food coloring, ability
    to shake and squeeze the bags.
- what is the result: The sand inside the bags
    is evenly colored.

- entities:
 - entity name: bags
 - before: contains uncolored or unevenly
     colored sand and food coloring
 - after: contains evenly colored sand
 - entity name: sand
 - before: uncolored or unevenly colored
 - after: evenly colored
 - entity name: food_coloring
 - before: present in the bags
 - after: mixed evenly with the sand

Example 3:
action: melt_wax

text: Melt candle wax flakes or cubes in a
    double boiler. Set a can, jar, or another
    heat-proof container in a pot, and place
    your solid candle wax (soy or paraffin are
    most common) inside. Surround the container
    with water, filling the pot about halfway up
     the container, then heat the pot on medium
    heat to double boil the wax to melt it
    completely, stirring every minute or so to
    make sure it melts evenly.

pddl_action:
(:action melt_wax
 :parameters (?wax ?container ?pot ?heat_source
     ?water)
 :precondition (and (solid ?wax) (in ?wax ?
     container) (heatproof ?container) (in ?
     container ?pot) (in ?water ?pot) (cold ?
     water))
 :effect (and (liquid ?wax) (heated ?water)))

entity_state_inference:
- action name: melt_wax
- summarize action: This action involves melting
     solid candle wax using a double boiler
    method. The solid wax is placed in a heat-
    proof container, which is then placed in a
    pot filled with water. The pot is heated,
    and the wax is stirred until it melts
    completely.
- what is needed to do the action: The action
    requires solid wax, a heat-proof container,
    a pot, water, and a heat source.
- what is the result: The solid wax is melted
    into liquid wax.

- entities:
 - entity name: wax
 - before: solid
 - after: liquid
 - entity name: container
 - before: empty or containing solid wax
 - after: containing liquid wax
 - entity name: pot
 - before: empty or containing water and
     container with solid wax
 - after: containing water and container with
     liquid wax
 - entity name: water
 - before: cold or room temperature
 - after: heated
 - entity name: heat_source
 - before: off
 - after: on
```

D Prompts

For reproducibility, we provide the verbatim prompts that we used in the above experiments.

D.1 Prompt without ZPD

Could you fill out the below PDDL actions with the predicates based on the text?
All fields: parameters, precondition and effect, should have predicates.
For each action, do NOT change the name and do NOT drop the action and do NOT add more actions.
The output should be in correct PDDL format.

<wikiHow text and domain header>

here are the actions I want:
<insert_action_names>
here are the types I have:
<insert_types>
here are the predicates I have:
<insert_predicates>
here are the texts containing steps to <insert_goal>:
<insert_text>

Example Completion:

(:action clean_water
  :parameters (?player - human ?water - water)
  :precondition (inventory ?player ?water)
  :effect (treated ?water)
)

D.2 Prompt with ZPD

Could you fill out the below PDDL actions with the predicates based on the text? All fields: parameters, precondition and effect, should have

predicates.
For each action, do NOT change the name and do NOT drop the action and do NOT add more actions and:
First, summarize the action in a few sentences based on the text and provide its requirements and its aims if it has.
Next, identify ALL the entities involved in the action and describe whether it changed, unchanged, added, removed in the action in natural language.
Last, translate it into PDDL format. Check all the related entities are in the 'parameters'.

Please use this output format:
- action name: ...
- summarize action: ...
- what is needed to do the action: ...
- what is the result: ...

- entities:
- entity name: ...
- before: ...
- after: ...

- describe how to match it to relevant predicates step by step:
1. ...
2. ...

<wikiHow text and domain header>

here are the actions I want:
<insert_action_names>

here are the types I have:
<insert_types>

here are the predicates I have:
<insert_predicates>

here are the texts containing steps to <insert_goal>:
<insert_text>

Example Completion:
- action name: clean_water
- summarize action: The player cleans water in their inventory using heat from a fire.
- what is needed to do the action: The player must have untreated water in their inventory and be at a location with fire.
- what is the result: The player has treated water in their inventory.

- entities:
- entity name: player
- before: Having untreated water in inventory.
- after: Having treated water in inventory.
- entity name: water
- before: Untreated.
- after: Treated.

- describe how to match it to pddl relevant predicates step by step:
1. Check if the player has untreated water in their inventory.
2. Check if the player is at a location with a fire.
3. Replace untreated water with treated water in the player's inventory in the effect.

PDDL:
(:action clean_water
  :parameters (?player - human ?loc - location ?water - water)
  :precondition (and (at ?player ?loc) (inventory ?player ?water) (not (treated ?water)) (has_fire ?loc))
  :effect (treated ?water)
)

E Calculating Actions Equivalence

The distance between two actions can be divided to two parts:

1. The distance between parameters:

   We do not need to consider the specific parameter names; we only need to consider the parameter types. For each parameter in Action1, we iterate over the parameter list of Action2 to find the first parameter in Action2 with the same type. We use two hash maps, p1 and p2, to record these two parameters and their corresponding types. We increment the counter by 1, remove that parameter from the parameter list of Action2, and break from the current loop. After the iteration, we obtain the number of matching parameters, n. The distance between parameters can be calculated as $|$number of parameters in Action1 $- n| + |$number of parameters in Action2 $- n|$.

2. The distance between preconditions/effects:

   For each condition in Action1, we iterate over the condition list of Action2. The conditions can only match if they have the same predicate and the same number of parameters. We iterate over the parameters in these conditions and make the following judgments:

- If neither of the two current parameters has appeared before (in p1 and p2) and these parameters are not identical, they don't match.
- If the two parameters have different categories, they don't match.
- If the two parameters have the same categories and don't have an index, we consider them as the same parameter entity and give them the same index. We continue the iteration.
- If the two parameters already have indexes, we check if the indexes are equal. If they are not equal, they don't match. Otherwise, we continue the iteration.
- In any other case, they don't match.

If all parameters of the two conditions match, we increment n by 1. The distance between preconditions/effects can be calculated as $|$number of preconditions/effects in Action1 $- n| + |$number of preconditions/effects in Action2$- n|$.

Towards A Unified View of Answer Calibration for Multi-Step Reasoning

Shumin Deng[♣], Ningyu Zhang[♡*], Nay Oo[♣], Bryan Hooi[♣*]
[♣]National University of Singapore, NUS-NCS Joint Lab [♡]Zhejiang University
{shumin,nay.oo,dcsbhk}@nus.edu.sg, zhangningyu@zju.edu.cn

Abstract

Large Language Models (LLMs) employing Chain-of-Thought (CoT) prompting have broadened the scope for improving multi-step reasoning capabilities. We generally divide multi-step reasoning into two phases: *path generation* to generate the reasoning path(s); and *answer calibration* post-processing the reasoning path(s) to obtain a final answer. However, the existing literature lacks systematic analysis on different answer calibration approaches. In this paper, we summarize the taxonomy of recent answer calibration techniques and break them down into step-level and path-level strategies. We then conduct a thorough evaluation on these strategies from a unified view, systematically scrutinizing step-level and path-level answer calibration across multiple paths. Experimental results reveal that integrating the dominance of both strategies tends to derive optimal outcomes. Our study holds the potential to illuminate key insights for optimizing multi-step reasoning with answer calibration.

1 Introduction

Chain-of-Thought (CoT) prompting (Wei et al., 2022) has significantly improved multi-step reasoning capabilities of Large Language Models (LLMs) (Zhao et al., 2023b; Qiao et al., 2023). As seen from Figure 1, the process of multi-step reasoning generally contains two primary modules: *reasoning path generation* which generates one or multiple reasoning paths (Fu et al., 2023; Yao et al., 2023b); and *answer calibration* which post-processes the reasoning path(s) to calibrate the initial output (Wang et al., 2023f; Zhao et al., 2023a).

In practice, answer calibration is pluggable and can be integrated into path generation models. The answer calibration framework can be divided into step and path levels, applicable to single or multiple paths, as illustrated in Figure 1. For *step-level* answer calibration on a single path, the model rectifies errors in intermediate-step answers of a generated path (Zhao et al., 2023a). For *step-level* answer calibration on multiple paths, the model verifies each intermediate-step answer (Weng et al., 2023) or aggregates the correct step answers (Cao, 2023) from multiple paths. For *path-level* answer calibration on a single path, the model revises the entire rationale to obtain the correct answer (Baek et al., 2023). For *path-level* answer calibration on multiple paths, the model produces a result indicating the consensus of all candidate paths (Wang et al., 2023f; Yoran et al., 2023). As answer calibration can identify and rectify errors in the reasoning path, or even holistically utilize multiple candidate paths, it plays a vital role in multi-step reasoning to ensure a precise, consistent and reliable reasoning process (Pan et al., 2024).

However, we argue that the crucial factors driving the success of answer calibration strategies remain obscure, with a comprehensive systematic

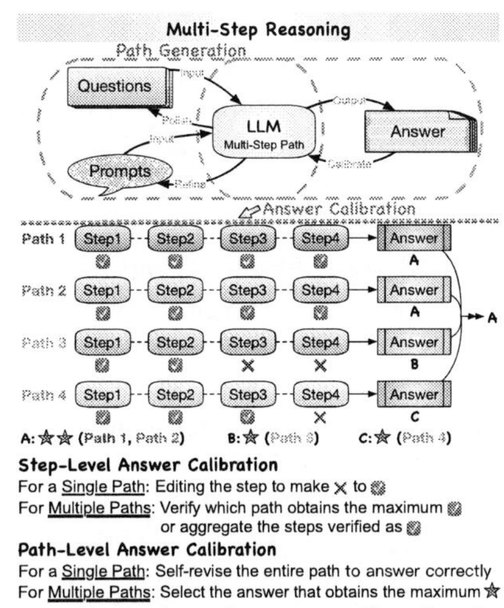

Figure 1: Illustration of answer calibration for multi-step reasoning with LLM. The methods of step/path-level answer calibration for *multiple paths* can employ answer calibration on *a single path* first. (Terminology clarification of answer calibration and model calibration is elaborated in Appendix A.)

* Corresponding Author.

Proceedings of the 2nd Workshop on Natural Language Reasoning and Structured Explanations (@ACL 2024), pages 25–38
August 15, 2024 ©2024 Association for Computational Linguistics

analysis still underexplored. To bridge the gap, our study investigates: (1) The specific conditions where answer calibration notably boosts multi-step reasoning performance; (2) The strengths and weaknesses of step-level versus path-level answer calibration, and the pathway to attaining optimal performance; (3) The robustness and generalizability of answer calibration strategies.

To address these questions, we dissect cutting-edge answer calibration techniques for multi-step reasoning with LLMs, and introduce a unified framework that elucidates step-level and path-level strategies. We define two thresholds to respectively signify the step-level and path-level dominance in the unified framework. We then undertake a comprehensive evaluation of answer calibration strategies, *w.r.t.* accuracy, faithfulness, informativeness, consistency, and perplexity over steps or paths. Through rigorous experiments on five representative multi-step reasoning tasks involving arithmetic (Ahn et al., 2024) and commonsense, we find that: **(1)** employing answer calibration can enhance accuracy, with the improvement being more noticeable in zero-shot scenarios (§4.2) and less significant on stronger backbone models (§4.4); **(2)** The optimal performance of the unified answer calibration strategy typically achieved by synthesizing step-level and path level dominance (§4.3); **(3)** path-level answer calibration is more beneficial in improving accuracy, and step-level answer calibration is more effective for mitigating low-quality prompting (§4.5); **(4)** answer calibration can improve consistency on arithmetic tasks but weakens faithfulness, informativeness and perplexity on both arithmetic and commonsense tasks (§4.6).

2 Related Work

Reasoning Path Generation. Previous methods for reasoning path generation mostly focus on two aspects to improve reasoning process, including refining input query or prompts (*input refinement*) and polishing the reasoning path (*rationale polish*).

As for *input refinement*, Zero-shot CoT (Kojima et al., 2022) and Few-shot CoT (Wei et al., 2022) are classic methods to elicit multi-step reasoning ability of LLMs, with "Let's think step by step" prompts. To decouple planning and execution, Wang et al. (2023d); Sun et al. (2024) devise a plan by prompting and divide and conquer multi-step tasks. To enrich prompts, Wang et al. (2024a) leverage structure triples as evidence, Kong et al. (2024) design role-play prompting, and Xu et al. (2023) employ re-reading instructions. Besides, LLM performance can also be affected by prompt complexity (Fu et al., 2023) and formats, such as program (Gao et al., 2023; Chen et al., 2023b; Sel et al., 2024; Jie et al., 2023; Lei and Deng, 2023; Bi et al., 2024) and table (Jin and Lu, 2023). Further, Wang et al. (2023b); Shi et al. (2023); Liang et al. (2024) propose to adaptively utilize prompts. Apart from refining prompts, Xi et al. (2023b) progressively refine the given questions, Wang et al. (2024d) convert semantically-wrapped questions to meta-questions, and Jie and Lu (2023) augment training data with program annotations.

In terms of *rationale polish*, recent work mainly focus on step-aware training (Wang et al., 2023g) and path-level optimization. For step-aware training, Zhang et al. (2023) introduce step-by-step planning and Lee and Kim (2023) recursively tackle intermediate steps; Jiang et al. (2023) reconstruct the reasoning rationale within prompts by residual connections; Paul et al. (2024) iteratively provide feedback on step answers; Lanchantin et al. (2023) leverage self-notes as intermediate steps and working memory; Li et al. (2023); Ling et al. (2023); Lightman et al. (2024) propose to verify on intermediate step answers; Li et al. (2024); Wang et al. (2023c) process step-aware verification by knowledge base retrieval. For path-level optimization, Li and Qiu (2023) enable LLMs to self-improve via pre-thinking and recalling relevant reasoning paths as memory; Wang et al. (2024b); Yue et al. (2024) leverage hybrid rationales in formats of natural language and program. Some work also generate deliberate rationales beyond CoT, such as Tree-of-Thought (Yao et al., 2023b; Long, 2023), Graph-of-Thought (Yao et al., 2023d; Besta et al., 2023) and Hypergraph-of-Thought (HoT) (Yao et al., 2023a).

Answer Calibration. Given generated reasoning path(s), answer calibration methods *post-process* the path(s) to calibrate the answer, involving step- or path-level calibration on one or multiple path(s).

Step-level answer calibration. Xue et al. (2023); Cao (2023) propose to rectify factual inconsistency and reasoning logic between intermediate steps. Miao et al. (2024); Wu et al. (2024) check the correctness of each intermediate step. Zhao et al. (2023a) post-edit multi-step reasoning paths with external knowledge. Yao et al. (2023c); Hao et al. (2023); Shinn et al. (2023); Yao et al. (2024); Chen et al. (2023a); Aksitov et al. (2023) draw up a plan and act step by step with LLMs as agents (Wang et al., 2024c; Xi et al., 2023a), encouraging interaction with the environment to provide feedback. Weng et al. (2023); Jiang et al. (2024) unleash the self-verification ability of LLMs, by forward reasoning and backward verification on intermediate step answers. Zhou et al. (2024) propose code-based self-verification on reasoning steps.

Path-level answer calibration. Zelikman et al. (2022) present a self-taught reasoner to iteratively generate rationales. Zheng et al. (2023) progressively use the generated answers as hints to make double-check. Mountantonakis and Tzitzikas (2023) enrich generated reasoning paths with hundreds of RDF KGs for fact checking. Baek et al. (2023) iteratively rectify errors in knowledge retrieval and answer generation for knowledge-augmented LMs. To cultivate the reasoning ability of smaller LMs, Ho et al. (2023); Wang et al. (2023e,h) propose to fine-tune CoT for knowledge distillation. Huang et al. (2023) demonstrate that LLMs can self-improve with high-confidence rationale-augmented answers. Yoran et al. (2023) prompt LLMs to meta-reason over multiple paths. Liu et al. (2023); Madaan et al. (2024) leverage feedback to improve model initial outputs. Wan et al. (2023) adaptively select in-context demonstrations from previous outputs to re-generate answers. Wang et al. (2023f) leverage self-consistency decoding strategy to majority vote on multiple path answers. Aggarwal and Yang (2023) propose adaptive-consistency to reduce sample budget.

3 Comprehensive Analysis of Answer Calibration

3.1 Formulation of Answer Calibration

Given a question denoted as $\mathcal{Q}$ and its associated prompt P, we leverage the LLM to generate the result $\mathcal{R}$. $\mathcal{R}$ can either encompass a single reasoning path $\mathcal{P}$ with an initial answer $\mathcal{A}$ or multiple reasoning paths $\mathbb{P} = \{\mathcal{P}_i\}_{i\in[1,N]}$ with a corresponding answer set $\mathbb{A} = \{\mathcal{A}_i\}_{i\in[1,N]}$. The total number of paths in $\mathbb{P}$ is N. In this paper, we analyze under the assumption that each reasoning path comprises a maximum of M steps. Paths exceeding M steps are truncated, and those with fewer steps are padded. The intermediate step answers for each reasoning path $\mathcal{P}_{(i)}$ are represented as $\{a_j\}^{(i)}_{j\in[1,M]}$.

Step-Level Answer Calibration. Given a single reasoning path $\mathcal{P}$ with an initial final path answer $\mathcal{A}$ and intermediate step answers $\{a_j\}_{j\in[1,M]}$, the objective of step-level answer calibration is to rectify any erroneous a_j, so that deriving the correct $\mathcal{A}$. For multiple reasoning paths $\mathbb{P}$, step-level answer calibration seeks to either select the reasoning path with the maximum correct intermediate step answers or aggregate the verified correct steps to form the most accurate reasoning path, leading to a correct final path answer. *Self-verification* (Weng et al., 2023) is an effective approach for step-level answer calibration on multiple reasoning paths.

Path-Level Answer Calibration. Given a single reasoning path $\mathcal{P}$ with an initial final path answer $\mathcal{A}$, the goal of path-level answer calibration is to revise the wrong $\mathcal{A}$. For multiple reasoning paths $\mathbb{P} = \{\mathcal{P}_i\}_{i\in[1,N]}$ with corresponding answers $\mathbb{A} = \{\mathcal{A}_i\}_{i\in[1,N]}$, path-level answer calibration is designed to select the reasoning path from $\mathbb{P}$ with the most consistent answer in $\mathbb{A}$. *Self-consistency* (Wang et al., 2023f) is a widely-used efficacious technique for path-level answer calibration on multiple reasoning paths.

3.2 Unified View of Answer Calibration

Considering the advantages of both step-level and path-level answer calibration, we propose to integrate the two strategies on multiple paths. Given the multiple generated reasoning paths $\mathbb{P} = \{\mathcal{P}_i\}_{i\in[1,N]}$, we define a unified score $\mathcal{D}_i$ for each $\mathcal{P}_i$ (with the final path answer: $\mathcal{A}_i$ and intermediate step answers: $\{a_j\}^{(i)}_{j\in[1,M]}$):

$$\mathcal{D}_i = \underbrace{\alpha\frac{n_i}{N}}_{path-level} + \underbrace{(1-\alpha)\frac{m_i}{M}}_{step-level} \quad (1)$$

where $n_i \in [1, N]$ is the frequency of $\mathcal{A}_i$ existing in $\mathbb{A}$, $m_i \in [0, M]$ is the number of correct intermediate steps in $\mathcal{P}_i$, and α is a hyper-parameter. *The final answer is $\mathcal{A}_{i^*}$ satisfying $i^* = \arg\max_{i\in[1,N]}(\mathcal{D}_i)$.*

To better analyze the effects of varying α in the unified framework, we then define particular choices for α which we call *step and path level dominant answer calibration*.

Definition 1. ***Step-Level Dominant Answer Calibration**: This choice refers to the level of α at which the step-level score is used as the dominant criterion, with the path-level score given much smaller weight and only serving to break ties when necessary. Specifically, larger m_i always results* *in larger $\mathcal{D}_i$, no matter how small n_i is. We denote this as: $\forall n_j, n_k \in [1, N]$ and $m_j, m_k \in [0, M]$, where $n_j < n_k$ and $m_j > m_k$, the scores D_j and D_k should satisfy*

$$\alpha\frac{n_j}{N} + (1-\alpha)\frac{m_j}{M} > \alpha\frac{n_k}{N} + (1-\alpha)\frac{m_k}{M}$$

Thus we can obtain

$$\alpha < \frac{1}{\frac{M(n_k - n_j)}{N(m_j - m_k)} + 1} \tag{2}$$

If Eq (2) is constant, we can infer that

$$\alpha < \min\left(\frac{1}{\frac{M(n_k-n_j)}{N(m_j-m_k)} + 1}\right) = \frac{1}{\frac{M\max(n_k-n_j)}{N\min(m_j-m_k)} + 1} \tag{3}$$

As $1 \leq n_j < n_k, n_j + n_k \leq N$, and $0 \leq m_k < m_j$, we can deduce that $\min(m_j - m_k) = 1$, $\max(n_k - n_j) = N - 2$. From the above, we deduce:

$$\alpha < \frac{1}{\frac{M(N-2)}{N} + 1} \tag{4}$$

Definition 2. ***Path-Level Dominant Answer Calibration****: For this choice, $\mathcal{D}_i$ gives priority to the path-level score, with the step-level score given much smaller weight and only serving to break ties when necessary. Concretely, larger n_i always conduces larger $\mathcal{D}_i$, no matter how small m_i is. We denote this as: $\forall n_j, n_k \in [1, N]$ and $m_j, m_k \in [0, M]$, where $n_j > n_k$ and $m_j < m_k$, the scores D_j and D_k should satisfy*

$$\alpha\frac{n_j}{N} + (1-\alpha)\frac{m_j}{M} > \alpha\frac{n_k}{N} + (1-\alpha)\frac{m_k}{M}$$

Analogously, we can obtain

$$\alpha > \frac{1}{\frac{M(n_j - n_k)}{N(m_k - m_j)} + 1} \tag{5}$$

If Eq (5) is constant, we can infer that

$$\alpha > \max\left(\frac{1}{\frac{M(n_j-n_k)}{N(m_k-m_j)} + 1}\right) = \frac{1}{\frac{M\min(n_j-n_k)}{N\max(m_k-m_j)} + 1} \tag{6}$$

As $1 \leq n_k < n_j$, and $0 \leq m_j < m_k \leq M$, we deduce that $\min(n_j - n_k) = 1$, $\max(m_k - m_j) = M - 0 = M$. From the above, we deduce:

$$\alpha > \frac{1}{\frac{1}{N} + 1} \tag{7}$$

In general, considering *step-level and path-level answer calibration dominance*, we can obtain two thresholds: $\frac{1}{\frac{M(N-2)}{N}+1}$ and $\frac{1}{\frac{1}{N}+1}$. Note that $\boldsymbol{\alpha = 0}$ **and** $\boldsymbol{\alpha = 1}$ **are respectively equivalent to the self-verification and self-consistency strategies.**

3.3 Evaluation of Answer Calibration

Calculation of `ROSCOE` Scores. In addition to the classical evaluation metric: Accuracy, Golovneva et al. (2023) have proposed **`ROSCOE`**, a suite of metrics for multi-step reasoning, under four perspectives: semantic alignment (`ROSCOE-SA`), semantic similarity (`ROSCOE-SS`), logical inference, and (`ROSCOE-LI`) and language coherence (`ROSCOE-LC`). Due to space limits, we select some representative scores from `ROSCOE` as evaluation metrics in the experiments.

Given source ground truth rationale ($\boldsymbol{s}$) and generated rationale ($\boldsymbol{h}$) with multiple steps (h_i), we calculate five scores (*All scores satisfy the principle that larger is better*):

(1) Faithfulness$_{step}$ ($\boldsymbol{h} \rightarrow \boldsymbol{s}$): To assess whether the model misconstrues the problem statement, or if the reasoning path is too nebulous, irrelevant, or improperly employs input information.

$$\textstyle\sum_{i=1}^{N} r\text{-align}(h_i \rightarrow \boldsymbol{s})/N \tag{8}$$

where N is the number of steps and r-align is used to measure how well $h_i \in \boldsymbol{h}$ can be aligned with any one of the steps in the ground truth path $\boldsymbol{s}$.

(2) Informativeness$_{path}$ ($\boldsymbol{h} \rightarrow \boldsymbol{s}$): To measure the level of concordance between the generated path and the source, and if the generated reasoning path is well-grounded with respect to the source.

$$[1 + \cos(\boldsymbol{h}, \boldsymbol{s})]/2 \tag{9}$$

where $\cos(\cdot,\cdot)$ is a function for cosine similarity.

(3) Consistency$_{steps}$ ($h_i \leftrightarrow h_j$): To measure logical entailment errors *within* the reasoning steps.

$$1 - \max_{i=2..N} \max_{j<i} p_{\text{contr}}(h_i, h_j) \tag{10}$$

where p_{contr} is used to assess the likelihood of step pairs contradicting each other. $h_i \in \boldsymbol{h}$ and $h_j \in \boldsymbol{h}$.

(4) Consistency$_{path}$ ($\boldsymbol{h} \leftrightarrow \boldsymbol{s}$): To evaluate mistakes in logical entailment between the generated reasoning path $\boldsymbol{h}$ and source context $\boldsymbol{s}$:

$$1 - \max_{i=1..N} \max_{j=1..T}\ p_{\text{contr}}(h_i, s_j) \tag{11}$$

where p_{contr} is the likelihood of source and generated steps contradicting each other. $s_j \in \boldsymbol{s}$; $h_i \in \boldsymbol{h}$.

(5) Perplexity$_{path}$ ($\boldsymbol{h}$): As an indicator of language coherence, it calculates average perplexity of all tokens in the generated reasoning path steps.

$$1/\text{PPL}(\boldsymbol{h}) \tag{12}$$

where PPL denotes the perplexity.

Task	Method	Accuracy ↑	Faithfulness ↑ (Over Steps)	Informativeness ↑ (Over Path)	Consistency ↑ (Within Steps)	Consistency ↑ (Within I/O)	Perplexity ↑ (Over Path)
GSM8K	CoT	80.21	88.73	96.38	**97.94**	96.94	9.14
	CoT + SV	82.34 (+2.13)	86.22 (−2.51)	95.19 (−1.19)	96.78 (−1.16)	93.46 (−3.48)	**14.90** (+5.76)
	CoT + SC	**87.11** (+6.90)	**88.83** (+0.10)	**96.40** (+0.02)~	97.90 (−0.04)~	**97.44** (+0.50)	8.90 (−0.24)
	ZS CoT	62.85	86.58	95.61	97.30	93.07	15.67
	ZS CoT + SV	67.70 (+4.85)	86.24 (−0.34)	95.19 (−0.42)	96.78 (−0.52)	93.44 (+0.37)	14.90 (−0.77)
	ZS CoT + SC	71.42 (+8.57)	86.70 (+0.12)	95.67 (+0.06)~	97.19 (−0.11)	94.57 (+1.50)	14.95 (−0.72)
SVAMP	CoT	78.20	**87.73**	**95.74**	30.57	9.82	**6.65**
	CoT + SV	**85.80** (+7.60)	87.26 (−0.47)	95.00 (−0.74)	33.39 (+2.82)	**10.41** (+0.59)	6.23 (−0.42)
	CoT + SC	84.40 (+6.20)	87.60 (−0.13)	95.71 (−0.03)	**33.51** (+2.94)	9.92 (+0.10)	6.22 (−0.43)
	ZS CoT	72.80	87.46	95.77	31.71	18.39	11.93
	ZS CoT + SV	81.20 (+8.40)	86.92 (−0.54)	95.05 (−0.72)	35.27 (+3.56)	20.24 (+1.85)	11.44 (−0.49)
	ZS CoT + SC	82.00 (+9.20)	87.40 (−0.06)	95.81 (+0.04)~	34.73 (+3.02)	19.67 (+1.28)	11.68 (−0.25)
MultiArith	CoT	97.67	**88.53**	**94.91**	7.77	7.47	5.51
	CoT + SV	**98.33** (+0.66)	88.36 (−0.17)	94.38 (−0.53)	**46.59** (+38.82)	**24.56** (+17.09)	**10.54** (+5.03)
	CoT + SC	98.17 (+0.50)	88.42 (−0.11)	94.82 (−0.09)	10.22 (+2.45)	9.29 (+1.82)	5.33 (−0.18)
	ZS CoT	87.00	89.32	95.30	47.54	24.39	10.75
	ZS CoT + SV	97.00 (+10.00)	88.35 (−0.97)	94.38 (−0.92)	46.26 (−1.28)	24.58 (+0.19)	10.54 (−0.21)
	ZS CoT + SC	97.00 (+10.00)	89.18 (−0.14)	95.32 (+0.02)~	47.42 (−0.12)	23.83 (−0.56)	10.63 (−0.12)
MathQA	CoT	52.83	**85.99**	**95.31**	49.57	23.78	**7.64**
	CoT + SV	**54.74** (+1.91)	85.93 (−0.06)	95.24 (−0.07)	51.39 (+1.82)	24.61 (+0.83)	7.18 (−0.46)
	CoT + SC	54.47 (+1.64)	85.93 (−0.06)	95.20 (−0.11)	**51.73** (+2.16)	**25.03** (+1.25)	7.15 (−0.49)
	ZS CoT	49.45	85.20	96.08	23.50	13.76	13.44
	ZS CoT + SV	52.86 (+3.41)	85.93 (+0.73)	95.24 (−0.84)	51.40 (+27.90)	24.63 (+10.87)	7.19 (−6.25)
	ZS CoT + SC	49.51 (+0.06)	85.22 (+0.02)~	96.08 (−0.00)~	23.66 (+0.16)	13.79 (+0.03)	13.48 (+0.04)~
CSQA	CoT	74.77	81.40	92.57	**95.57**	**57.54**	2.46
	CoT + SV	74.04 (−0.73)	80.89 (−0.51)	92.10 (−0.47)	92.77 (−2.80)	56.05 (−1.49)	**2.47** (+0.01)~
	CoT + SC	**75.27** (+0.50)	**81.50** (+0.10)	**92.71** (+0.14)	95.04 (−0.53)	56.97 (−0.57)	2.43 (−0.03)
	ZS CoT	67.57	79.77	95.26	25.81	29.17	9.90
	ZS CoT + SV	66.42 (−1.15)	79.06 (−0.71)	94.65 (−0.61)	25.36 (−0.45)	28.56 (−0.61)	9.06 (−0.84)
	ZS CoT + SC	71.58 (+4.01)	79.51 (−0.26)	95.21 (−0.05)~	25.08 (−0.73)	29.69 (+0.52)	8.96 (−0.94)

Table 1: Comprehensive performance (%) with different strategies on GPT-3.5 (`gpt-3.5-turbo`). **CoT**: Few-shot CoT (Wei et al., 2022) with complex-prompting (Fu et al., 2023); **ZS-CoT**: Zero-Shot CoT (Kojima et al., 2022); **SV**: Self-Verification (Weng et al., 2023); **SC**: Self-Consistency (Wang et al., 2023f). **Best few-shot results** are marked in **bold**; best *zero-shot* results are underlined. I/O: input/output. ↑: larger is better. ~, ~: comparable.

4 Experiments

4.1 Setup

Evaluation Metrics. In this paper, we aim to conduct comprehensive evaluation on multi-step reasoning, thus we select some scores from ROSCOE (Golovneva et al., 2023) as introduced in §3.3, which contains a suite of metrics allowing us to evaluate the quality of reasoning rationales, not limited to the correctness of final answers.

Datasets. We evaluate on five benchmark datasets involving arithmetic and commonsense multi-step reasoning: **GSM8K** (Cobbe et al., 2021), **SVAMP** (Patel et al., 2021), **MultiArith** (Roy and Roth, 2015), **MathQA** (Amini et al., 2019) and **CSQA** (Talmor et al., 2019).

Models. For reasoning *path generation*, we leverage **Zero-shot CoT (ZS CoT)** (Kojima et al., 2022) and **Few-shot CoT (CoT)** (Wei et al., 2022) with complexity-based prompting (Fu et al., 2023). For *answer calibration*, we employ **Self-Verification (SV)** (Weng et al., 2023) and **Self-Consistency (SC)** (Wang et al., 2023f) on multiple paths. SV is a step-level strategy, which verifies intermediate-step answers and returns the path containing the maximum number of correct step answers. SC is a path-level strategy, which conducts majority voting on final answers of all generated paths and selects the most consistent result.

Implementation. We release the codes and generated results anonymously[1]. In this paper, the number of reasoning paths N defined in Eq (1) is 10, and number of intermediate steps M is 3 on all datasets except for CSQA where M is 10. We utilize GPT-3.5 with `gpt-3.5-turbo` engine as the backbone LLM to generate reasoning paths (the model choice justification is elaborated in Appendix B), and the temperature is set to 0.7. We also leverage GPT-4 (OpenAI, 2023) with `gpt-4` engine to generate ground-truth rationales given the ground-truth answers for all datasets excluding GSM8K (which already contains them). For evaluation referring to ROSCOE (Golovneva et al., 2023), we respectively lever-

[1] https://github.com/231sm/Eval_Multi-Step_Reasoning.

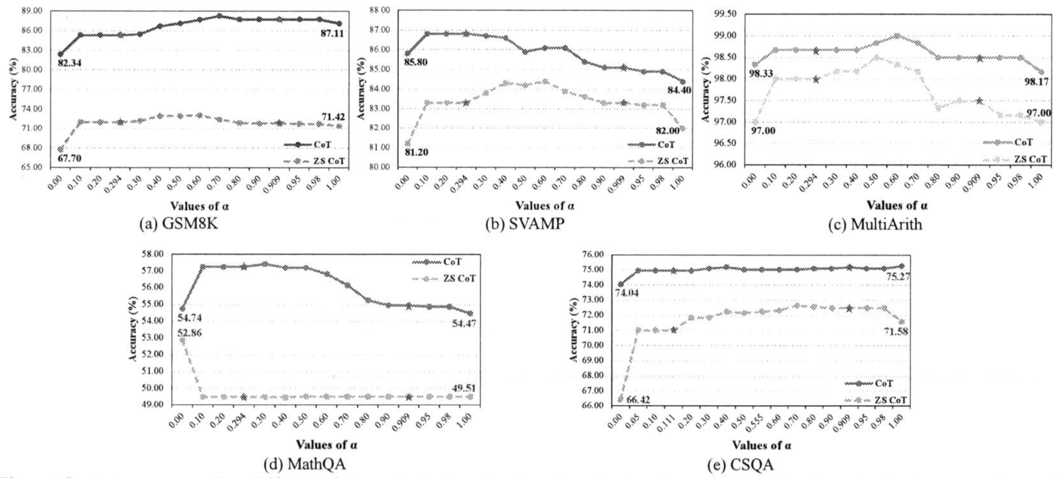

Figure 2: Accuracy under different integrated *step-level* and *path-level* answer calibration strategies, varying with the values of α defined in Eq (1). Performance with two thresholds of $\frac{1}{\frac{M(N-2)}{N}+1}$ and $\frac{1}{\frac{1}{N}+1}$ are marked as ★.

age `all-MiniLM-L6-v2`/*SentenceTransformer*, and pretrained `gpt2-large` (Radford et al., 2019) to obtain token/sentence embedding and calculate perplexity defined in Eq (12). All the reasoning paths for CoT and ZS CoT were generated during 8th to 23rd June 2023, and answer calibration on the generated reasoning paths was conducted during 12th October to 8th November 2023.

4.2 Analysis on Step-Level and Path-Level Answer Calibration Strategies

We respectively incorporate the effective step-level and path-level answer calibration strategies, Self-Verification (SV) and Self-Consistency (SC), into CoT-based models operating on multiple paths. We evaluate their performance using six evaluation metrics, with the results presented in Table 1.

Generally, **in terms of *accuracy*, employing answer calibration is effective.** Seen from Table 1, we find that models equipped with SV and SC obviously outperform vanilla methods, as both few-shot and zero-shot CoT employing SV/SC achieve significant accuracy improvements on almost all tasks. Notably, zero-shot CoT with SV and SC achieves much more significant outperformance of accuracy than few-shot settings on almost all tasks, demonstrating that **answer calibration is more effective in zero-shot settings**. As zero-shot CoT is relatively challenging due to the absence of task-specific in-context learning, answer calibration strategies essentially creating a feedback loop where the model assesses its own performance and adjusts accordingly, could help to mitigate biases and overfitting to specific patterns during inference, allowing the model to better generalize to new types of problems and datasets.

Furthermore, **in terms of *other metrics*, answer calibration can improve *consistency* on arithmetic tasks but weakens *faithfulness*, *informativeness* and *perplexity* on both arithmetic and commonsense tasks.** Observed from Table 1, we find that SV and SC weaken the *perplexity* score (16 out of 20 cases), suggesting that the rationale generated from multiple paths is more complex than that from a single path with CoT models. However, these two strategies improve *consistency* scores on arithmetic tasks (10 out of 16 cases; 14 out of 16 cases), intuitively benefiting from multiple paths. As SV verifies answers for intermediate steps and SC considers answers for all paths, they naturally enhance consistency within steps and between input/output (I/O). Additionally, SV and SC worsen *faithfulness* and *informativeness* on almost all tasks (15 out of 20 cases for both). The possible reason is that answer calibration on multiple paths focuses more on answer accuracy, while its increased complexity of its rationales tends to result in lower alignment and concordance between the source content and the output path. Generally, despite the benefits of employing SV and SC to CoT-based methods, the improvements are task-dependent and vary across different metrics.

4.3 Analysis on Unified Answer Calibration Strategies

We then integrate step-level and path-level answer calibration strategies, varying α as defined in Eq (1). We present the accuracy of the unified strategies in Figure 2. As observed, accuracy peaks at a specific value of α between the two thresholds

Engine	Strategy	GSM8K	SVAMP	MultiArith	CSQA
GPT-3 (175B) `code-davinci-001`	CoT	13.84	38.42	45.85	46.75
	CoT + SV	13.92↑	38.96↑	46.19↑	47.68↑
	CoT + SC	23.40⇑	54.58⇑	79.82⇑	54.92⇑
	CoT + SC + SV	23.59⇑	54.68⇑	80.01⇑	55.09⇑
Instruct-GPT (175B) `code-davinci-002`	CoT	60.81	75.87	96.13	77.42
	CoT + SV	65.14⇑	76.99↑	99.15⇑	77.83↑
	CoT + SC	78.00⇑	86.77⇑	100.00⇑	81.43⇑
	CoT + SC + SV	78.32⇑	86.94⇑	100.00⇑	81.53⇑
GPT-3.5 `gpt-3.5-turbo`	CoT	80.21	78.20	97.67	74.77
	CoT + SV	82.34↑	85.80⇑	98.33↑	74.04↓
	CoT + SC	87.11⇑	84.40⇑	98.17↑	75.27↑
	CoT + SC + SV	88.25⇑	86.80⇑	99.00↑	75.18↑

Table 2: Accuracy (%) with different backbone engines. ↑/⇑: slightly/significantly better; ↓: slightly worse than the baseline few-shot CoT. We refer to Weng et al. (2023) for results with GPT-3 and Instruct-GPT engines. As Weng et al. (2023) didn't test on MathQA dataset, we also exclude the results of MathQA here for fair comparisons.

defined in Eq (4) and (7) in almost all scenarios across all tasks (*i.e.*, 8 out of 10 cases), demonstrating that **optimal model performance should balance both step-level and path-level answer calibration dominance**. Besides, we notice that for "CoT on SVAMP task" in Figure 2(b) and "zero-shot CoT on MathQA task" Figure 2(d), employing integrated answer calibration strategies reaches a peak with α not between the two thresholds, and the overall performance remains stably lower than the initial best accuracy with $\alpha = 0$ (*i.e.*, SV). The possible reason may related to *employing SV* (i.e., $\alpha = 0$) *presenting more significant advantages than SC* (i.e., $\alpha = 1$) *in the two scenarios*. Specifically, CoT on SVAMP respectively achieves accuracy of 85.80% and 84.40% when α values 0 (SV) and 1 (SC), with the difference larger than 1%; Zero-shot CoT on MathQA employing SV and SC achieves accuracy of 52.86% v.s. 49.51%, where the difference is larger than 3%. Except for these two distinctive scenarios, others in Figure 2 obtain the optimal results by synthesizing step-level and path level answer calibration dominance.

In conclusion, the value of α plays a significant role in the performance of both few-shot and zero-shot CoT. Optimal ranges of α for each task are mostly between the two thresholds of step-level and path-level answer calibration dominance. The marked two thresholds represent boundaries for optimizing performance, which could guide further fine-tuning. Besides, the performance variance across datasets implies that the characteristics of each task, such as complexity, size, or the nature of the tasks. Models equipped with answer calibration strategies may require task-specific tuning to achieve the best performance.

4.4 Effects of Backbone Models

We compare accuracy on CoT-based answer calibration strategies with different LLM backbone engines, and present results in Table 2.

As observed from the results, for GPT-3 and Instruct-GPT, both self-verification (SV) and self-consistency (SC) provide consistent improvements; while on the larger GPT-3.5 model, their improvements are observably weaker, particularly for SV, with which accuracy even slightly drops on the CSQA task. The possible reason is that GPT-3.5 is more prone to making mistakes when verifying on intermediate-step answers for multiple paths. Further, for integrated answer calibration strategies (SV+SC), the model's performance is close to the better one between SV and SC. Generally, path-level answer calibration is more advantageous than step-level one, with relatively higher accuracy and lower computation cost. Based on these observations, we can infer that **answer calibration strategies, especially path-level self-consistency, provide benefits in many cases, particularly on less powerful LLMs**.

We further speculate, if the path generation for CoT with strong backbone LLM is sophisticated enough, the answer calibration may be simplified. We can directly conduct *path-level* answer calibration for multiple paths. But these findings cannot indicate that step-level answer calibration is meaningless for stronger backbone LLMs. As seen from Table 1, LLM equipped with step-level answer calibration is relatively beneficial to improve consistency scores. Besides, as mentioned in Weng et al. (2023), step-level answer calibration can provide explainable answers by verifying on intermediate-step answers, making results more reliable.

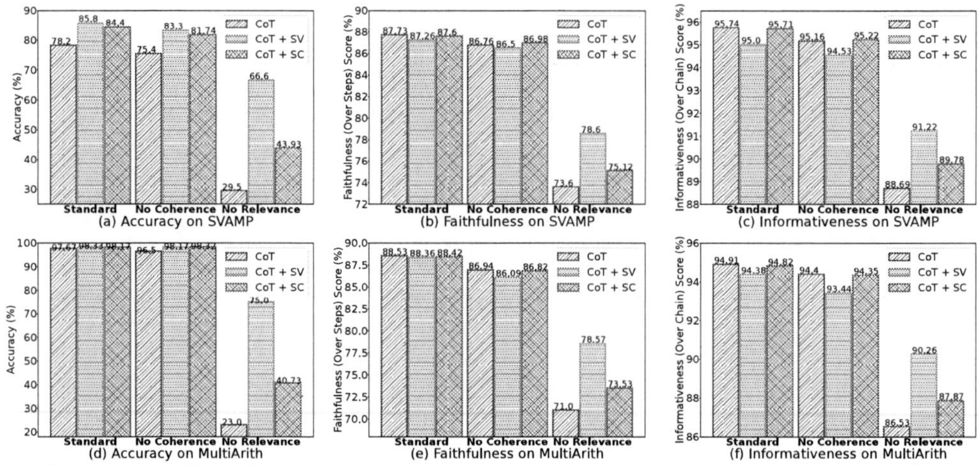

Figure 3: Performance (%) of "*Accuracy, Faithfulness (Over Steps)* and *Informativeness (Over Path)*" on SVAMP and MultiArith with different prompting on CoT models. We didn't show full results of other tasks for space limits.

4.5 Effects of Prompting

We further demonstrate the effects of prompting with few-shot demonstrations on answer calibration, evaluated on CoT models.

We respectively input prompts of *no coherence* and *no relevance* for few-shot CoT referring to Wang et al. (2023a) (examples are listed in Appendix C), and present performance on SVAMP and MultiArith in Figure 3. As seen, the deficiency of coherence and relevance in the prompting observably weaken the performance of all models, with no relevance having a more profound impact than no coherence. In addition, CoT+SV achieves comparable performance with CoT+SC when prompting is standard or not coherent. Further, CoT+SV tends to perform observably better than CoT+SC, when prompting with no relevance, indicating that step-level answer calibration strategy SV, is beneficial to maintain performance under adverse conditions. This observation suggests **the robustness of step-level answer calibration**. It also highlights **the potential benefits of step-level answer calibration strategies to mitigate performance degeneration caused by poor prompting**. The possible reason is that step-level answer calibration strategies break down the task into subtasks, and these subtasks are simple enough so that less likely to be influenced by the low-quality prompts.

4.6 Analysis on Tasks

As seen from Table 1,2, and Figure 2, generally, **SV and SC present more significant outperformance on arithmetic tasks than on the commonsense task (CSQA)**. Further, for CSQA, employing answer calibration tends to worsen the consistency scores, which is contrary to the trend observed in arithmetic tasks. The possible explanation lies in the characteristics of each task, such as complexity, size, or the nature of the tasks. In the CSQA task, correct intermediate steps may not always contribute to a coherent reasoning path due to potential irrelevance and redundancy. Specifically, even if we calibrate both intermediate step and path answers, there can be some correct commonsense statements while irrelevant to the question, resulting in worse consistency and perplexity. Conversely, in arithmetic tasks, correct intermediate answers almost guarantee a consistent reasoning path, as all intermediate answers are necessary and will contribute to a correct final answer.

5 Conclusion and Future Work

In this paper, we dissect multi-step reasoning into path generation and answer calibration, and provide a unified view of answer calibration strategies through a comprehensive evaluation. We find that path-level answer calibration is particularly potent in improving accuracy, while step-level answer calibration is more suitable for addressing issues related to low-quality prompting. The improvement is more pronounced in zero-shot scenarios and less significant on stronger backbone models. We also define step-level and path-level answer calibration dominance with two thresholds, and propose to integrate of the two types of strategies, which is promising to achieve optimal performance. Our findings suggest that answer calibration is a versatile strategy that can be integrated into various models to bolster multi-step reasoning capabilities of LLMs. In the future, we aim to develop more sophisticated multi-step reasoning models, drawing on the insights and conclusions from this study.

Limitations

The main limitation for this paper is that we didn't analyze more answer calibration strategies, such as step-/path-level methods on the single path, and varying the numbers of steps and paths in the unified answer calibration strategies. Besides, we can also employ answer calibration strategies to other path generation models, not limited to CoT-based methods. Further, we should also evaluate answer calibration strategies on more tasks to make the results more sufficient.

Broader Impact

Technical Novelty Emphasis. We have conducted an empirical study of answer calibration and proposed a unified method to address that *Step-Level / Path-Level Answer Calibration* for *a Single or Multiple Paths* can be integrated together, with the two thresholds of *Step-/Path-Level Dominant Answer Calibration* and a hyper-parameter α. Our analysis has the potential to inspire further research and practical implications on unified answer calibration, such as *"how the hyper-parameter α can be optimally chosen across different tasks, like iterative tuning"*. Our paper is based on an empirical study, and its main contributions are to unify multiple seemingly disparate types of approaches into a common framework, allowing us to investigate empirical questions to obtain more insights, *e.g.*,

(1) Employing answer calibration can enhance accuracy, with the improvement being more noticeable in zero-shot scenarios and less significant on stronger backbone models;

(2) The optimal performance of the unified answer calibration strategy typically achieved by synthesizing step-level and path level dominance;

(3) Path-level answer calibration is more beneficial in improving accuracy, and step-level answer calibration is more effective for mitigating low-quality prompting;

(4) Answer calibration can improve consistency on arithmetic tasks but weakens faithfulness, informativeness and perplexity on both arithmetic and commonsense tasks.

Acknowledgment

We would like to express gratitude to the anonymous reviewers for their kind and helpful comments. This work was supported by the National Natural Science Foundation of China (No. 62206246), the Fundamental Research Funds for the Central Universities (226-2023-00138), Zhejiang Provincial Natural Science Foundation of China (No. LGG22F030011), Yongjiang Talent Introduction Programme (2021A-156-G), Tencent AI Lab Rhino-Bird Focused Research Program (RBFR2024003), Information Technology Center and State Key Lab of CAD&CG, Zhejiang University, and NUS-NCS Joint Laboratory (A-0008542-00-00).

References

Aman Madaan Pranjal Aggarwal and Mausam Yiming Yang. 2023. Let's sample step by step: Adaptive-consistency for efficient reasoning and coding with llms. In *EMNLP*, pages 12375–12396. Association for Computational Linguistics.

Janice Ahn, Rishu Verma, Renze Lou, Di Liu, Rui Zhang, and Wenpeng Yin. 2024. Large language models for mathematical reasoning: Progresses and challenges. In *EACL (Student Research Workshop)*, pages 225–237. Association for Computational Linguistics.

Renat Aksitov, Sobhan Miryoosefi, Zonglin Li, Daliang Li, Sheila Babayan, Kavya Kopparapu, Zachary Fisher, Ruiqi Guo, Sushant Prakash, Pranesh Srinivasan, Manzil Zaheer, Felix Yu, and Sanjiv Kumar. 2023. Rest meets react: Self-improvement for multi-step reasoning llm agent. *CoRR*, abs/2312.10003.

Aida Amini, Saadia Gabriel, Shanchuan Lin, Rik Koncel-Kedziorski, Yejin Choi, and Hannaneh Hajishirzi. 2019. Mathqa: Towards interpretable math word problem solving with operation-based formalisms. In *NAACL-HLT (1)*, pages 2357–2367. Association for Computational Linguistics.

Jinheon Baek, Soyeong Jeong, Minki Kang, Jong Park, and Sung Ju Hwang. 2023. Knowledge-augmented language model verification. In *EMNLP*, pages 1720–1736. Association for Computational Linguistics.

Maciej Besta, Nils Blach, Ales Kubicek, Robert Gerstenberger, Lukas Gianinazzi, Joanna Gajda, Tomasz Lehmann, Michal Podstawski, Hubert Niewiadomski, Piotr Nyczyk, and Torsten Hoefler. 2023. Graph of thoughts: Solving elaborate problems with large language models. *CoRR*, abs/2308.09687.

Zhen Bi, Ningyu Zhang, Yinuo Jiang, Shumin Deng, Guozhou Zheng, and Huajun Chen. 2024. When do program-of-thoughts work for reasoning? In *AAAI*. AAAI Press.

Lang Cao. 2023. Graphreason: Enhancing reasoning capabilities of large language models through a graph-based verification approach. *CoRR*, abs/2308.09267.

Baian Chen, Chang Shu, Ehsan Shareghi, Nigel Collier, Karthik Narasimhan, and Shunyu Yao. 2023a. Fireact: Toward language agent fine-tuning. *CoRR*, abs/2310.05915.

Wenhu Chen, Xueguang Ma, Xinyi Wang, and William W. Cohen. 2023b. Program of thoughts prompting: Disentangling computation from reasoning for numerical reasoning tasks. *Transactions on Machine Learning Research*.

Karl Cobbe, Vineet Kosaraju, Mohammad Bavarian, Jacob Hilton, Reiichiro Nakano, Christopher Hesse, and John Schulman. 2021. Training verifiers to solve math word problems. *CoRR*, abs/2110.14168.

Yao Fu, Hao Peng, Ashish Sabharwal, Peter Clark, and Tushar Khot. 2023. Complexity-based prompting for multi-step reasoning. In *ICLR*. OpenReview.net.

Luyu Gao, Aman Madaan, Shuyan Zhou, Uri Alon, Pengfei Liu, Yiming Yang, Jamie Callan, and Graham Neubig. 2023. PAL: program-aided language models. In *ICML*, volume 202 of *Proceedings of Machine Learning Research*, pages 10764–10799. PMLR.

Olga Golovneva, Moya Peng Chen, S pencer Poff, Martin Corredor, Luke Zettlemoyer, Maryam Fazel-Zarandi, and Asli Celikyilmaz. 2023. ROSCOE: A suite of metrics for scoring step-by-step reasoning. In *The Eleventh International Conference on Learning Representations*.

Chuan Guo, Geoff Pleiss, Yu Sun, and Kilian Q. Weinberger. 2017. On calibration of modern neural networks. In *ICML*, volume 70 of *Proceedings of Machine Learning Research*, pages 1321–1330. PMLR.

Shibo Hao, Yi Gu, Haodi Ma, Joshua Jiahua Hong, Zhen Wang, Daisy Zhe Wang, and Zhiting Hu. 2023. Reasoning with language model is planning with world model. In *EMNLP*, pages 8154–8173. Association for Computational Linguistics.

Namgyu Ho, Laura Schmid, and Se-Young Yun. 2023. Large language models are reasoning teachers. In *ACL (1)*, pages 14852–14882. Association for Computational Linguistics.

Jiaxin Huang, Shixiang Gu, Le Hou, Yuexin Wu, Xuezhi Wang, Hongkun Yu, and Jiawei Han. 2023. Large language models can self-improve. In *EMNLP*, pages 1051–1068. Association for Computational Linguistics.

Song Jiang, Zahra Shakeri, Aaron Chan, Maziar Sanjabi, Hamed Firooz, Yinglong Xia, Bugra Akyildiz, Yizhou Sun, Jinchao Li, Qifan Wang, and Asli Celikyilmaz. 2023. Resprompt: Residual connection prompting advances multi-step reasoning in large language models. *CoRR*, abs/2310.04743.

Weisen Jiang, Han Shi, Longhui Yu, Zhengying Liu, Yu Zhang, Zhenguo Li, and James T. Kwok. 2024. Forward-backward reasoning in large language models for mathematical verification. In *ACL (Findings)*. Association for Computational Linguistics.

Zhanming Jie and Wei Lu. 2023. Leveraging training data in few-shot prompting for numerical reasoning. In *ACL (Findings)*, pages 10518–10526. Association for Computational Linguistics.

Zhanming Jie, Trung Quoc Luong, Xinbo Zhang, Xiaoran Jin, and Hang Li. 2023. Design of chain-of-thought in math problem solving. *CoRR*, abs/2309.11054.

Ziqi Jin and Wei Lu. 2023. Tab-cot: Zero-shot tabular chain of thought. In *ACL (Findings)*, pages 10259–10277. Association for Computational Linguistics.

Takeshi Kojima, Shixiang Shane Gu, Machel Reid, Yutaka Matsuo, and Yusuke Iwasawa. 2022. Large language models are zero-shot reasoners. In *NeurIPS*.

Aobo Kong, Shiwan Zhao, Hao Chen, Qicheng Li, Yong Qin, Ruiqi Sun, Xin Zhou, Enzhi Wang, and Xiaohang Dong. 2024. Better zero-shot reasoning with role-play prompting. In *NAACL (1)*. Association for Computational Linguistics.

Jack Lanchantin, Shubham Toshniwal, Jason Weston, Arthur Szlam, and Sainbayar Sukhbaatar. 2023. Learning to reason and memorize with self-notes. In *NeurIPS*.

Soochan Lee and Gunhee Kim. 2023. Recursion of thought: A divide-and-conquer approach to multi-context reasoning with language models. In *ACL (Findings)*, pages 623–658. Association for Computational Linguistics.

IokTong Lei and Zhidong Deng. 2023. Selfzcot: a self-prompt zero-shot cot from semantic-level to code-level for a better utilization of llms. *CoRR*, abs/2305.11461.

Xiaonan Li and Xipeng Qiu. 2023. Mot: Memory-of-thought enables chatgpt to self-improve. In *EMNLP*, pages 6354–6374. Association for Computational Linguistics.

Xingxuan Li, Ruochen Zhao, Yew Ken Chia, Bosheng Ding, Lidong Bing, Shafiq R. Joty, and Soujanya Poria. 2024. Chain of knowledge: A framework for grounding large language models with structured knowledge bases. In *ICLR*. OpenReview.net.

Yifei Li, Zeqi Lin, Shizhuo Zhang, Qiang Fu, Bei Chen, Jian-Guang Lou, and Weizhu Chen. 2023. Making language models better reasoners with step-aware verifier. In *ACL (1)*, pages 5315–5333. Association for Computational Linguistics.

Zhenwen Liang, Dian Yu, Xiaoman Pan, Wenlin Yao, Qingkai Zeng, Xiangliang Zhang, and Dong Yu. 2024. Mint: Boosting generalization in mathematical reasoning via multi-view fine-tuning. In *LREC/COLING*, pages 11307–11318. ELRA and ICCL.

Hunter Lightman, Vineet Kosaraju, Yura Burda, Harrison Edwards, Bowen Baker, Teddy Lee, Jan Leike, John Schulman, Ilya Sutskever, and Karl Cobbe. 2024. Let's verify step by step. In *ICLR*. OpenReview.net.

Zhan Ling, Yunhao Fang, Xuanlin Li, Zhiao Huang, Mingu Lee, Roland Memisevic, and Hao Su. 2023. Deductive verification of chain-of-thought reasoning. In *NeurIPS*.

Hao Liu, Carmelo Sferrazza, and Pieter Abbeel. 2023. Chain of hindsight aligns language models with feedback. *CoRR*, abs/2302.02676.

Jieyi Long. 2023. Large language model guided tree-of-thought. *CoRR*, abs/2305.08291.

Aman Madaan, Niket Tandon, Prakhar Gupta, Skyler Hallinan, Luyu Gao, Sarah Wiegreffe, Uri Alon, Nouha Dziri, Shrimai Prabhumoye, Yiming Yang, Sean Welleck, Bodhisattwa Prasad Majumder, Katherine Hermann, Shashank Gupta, Amir Yazdanbakhsh, and Peter Clark. 2024. Self-refine: Iterative refinement with self-feedback. In *ICLR*. OpenReview.net.

Ning Miao, Yee Whye Teh, and Tom Rainforth. 2024. Selfcheck: Using llms to zero-shot check their own step-by-step reasoning. In *ICLR*. OpenReview.net.

Michalis Mountantonakis and Yannis Tzitzikas. 2023. Using multiple RDF knowledge graphs for enriching chatgpt responses. In *ECML/PKDD (7)*, volume 14175 of *Lecture Notes in Computer Science*, pages 324–329. Springer.

Alexandru Niculescu-Mizil and Rich Caruana. 2005. Predicting good probabilities with supervised learning. In *ICML*, volume 119 of *ACM International Conference Proceeding Series*, pages 625–632. ACM.

OpenAI. 2023. GPT-4 technical report. *OpenAI*.

Liangming Pan, Michael Saxon, Wenda Xu, Deepak Nathani, Xinyi Wang, and William Yang Wang. 2024. Automatically correcting large language models: Surveying the landscape of diverse automated correction strategies. *Transactions of the Association for Computational Linguistics*, 12:484–506.

Arkil Patel, Satwik Bhattamishra, and Navin Goyal. 2021. Are NLP models really able to solve simple math word problems? In *NAACL-HLT*, pages 2080–2094. Association for Computational Linguistics.

Debjit Paul, Mete Ismayilzada, Maxime Peyrard, Beatriz Borges, Antoine Bosselut, Robert West, and Boi Faltings. 2024. REFINER: reasoning feedback on intermediate representations. In *EACL (1)*, pages 1100–1126. Association for Computational Linguistics.

Shuofei Qiao, Yixin Ou, Ningyu Zhang, Xiang Chen, Yunzhi Yao, Shumin Deng, Chuanqi Tan, Fei Huang, and Huajun Chen. 2023. Reasoning with language model prompting: A survey. In *ACL (1)*, pages 5368–5393. Association for Computational Linguistics.

Alec Radford, Jeff Wu, Rewon Child, David Luan, Dario Amodei, and Ilya Sutskever. 2019. Language models are unsupervised multitask learners. *OpenAI*.

Subhro Roy and Dan Roth. 2015. Solving general arithmetic word problems. In *EMNLP*, pages 1743–1752. The Association for Computational Linguistics.

Bilgehan Sel, Ahmad Al-Tawaha, Vanshaj Khattar, Lu Wang, Ruoxi Jia, and Ming Jin. 2024. Algorithm of thoughts: Enhancing exploration of ideas in large language models. In *ICML*, Proceedings of Machine Learning Research. PMLR.

Fobo Shi, Peijun Qing, Dong Yang, Nan Wang, Youbo Lei, Haonan Lu, and Xiaodong Lin. 2023. Prompt space optimizing few-shot reasoning success with large language models. *CoRR*, abs/2306.03799.

Noah Shinn, Federico Cassano, Edward Berman, Ashwin Gopinath, Karthik Narasimhan, and Shunyu Yao. 2023. Reflexion: Language agents with verbal reinforcement learning. In *NeurIPS*.

Simeng Sun, Yang Liu, Shuohang Wang, Dan Iter, Chenguang Zhu, and Mohit Iyyer. 2024. PEARL: prompting large language models to plan and execute actions over long documents. In *EACL (1)*, pages 469–486. Association for Computational Linguistics.

Alon Talmor, Jonathan Herzig, Nicholas Lourie, and Jonathan Berant. 2019. Commonsenseqa: A question answering challenge targeting commonsense knowledge. In *NAACL-HLT (1)*, pages 4149–4158. Association for Computational Linguistics.

Katherine Tian, Eric Mitchell, Allan Zhou, Archit Sharma, Rafael Rafailov, Huaxiu Yao, Chelsea Finn, and Christopher D. Manning. 2023. Just ask for calibration: Strategies for eliciting calibrated confidence scores from language models fine-tuned with human feedback. In *EMNLP*, pages 5433–5442. Association for Computational Linguistics.

Xingchen Wan, Ruoxi Sun, Hanjun Dai, Sercan Ö. Arik, and Tomas Pfister. 2023. Better zero-shot reasoning with self-adaptive prompting. In *ACL (Findings)*, pages 3493–3514. Association for Computational Linguistics.

Boshi Wang, Sewon Min, Xiang Deng, Jiaming Shen, You Wu, Luke Zettlemoyer, and Huan Sun. 2023a. Towards understanding chain-of-thought prompting: An empirical study of what matters. In *ACL (1)*, pages 2717–2739. Association for Computational Linguistics.

Jianing Wang, Qiushi Sun, Nuo Chen, Xiang Li, and Ming Gao. 2024a. Boosting language models reasoning with chain-of-knowledge prompting. In *ACL*. Association for Computational Linguistics.

Jinyuan Wang, Junlong Li, and Hai Zhao. 2023b. Self-prompted chain-of-thought on large language models for open-domain multi-hop reasoning. In *EMNLP (Findings)*, pages 2717–2731. Association for Computational Linguistics.

Ke Wang, Houxing Ren, Aojun Zhou, Zimu Lu, Sichun Luo, Weikang Shi, Renrui Zhang, Linqi Song, Mingjie Zhan, and Hongsheng Li. 2024b. Mathcoder: Seamless code integration in llms for enhanced mathematical reasoning. In *ICLR*. OpenReview.net.

Keheng Wang, Feiyu Duan, Sirui Wang, Peiguang Li, Yunsen Xian, Chuantao Yin, Wenge Rong, and Zhang Xiong. 2023c. Knowledge-driven cot: Exploring faithful reasoning in llms for knowledge-intensive question answering. *CoRR*, abs/2308.13259.

Lei Wang, Chen Ma, Xueyang Feng, Zeyu Zhang, Hao Yang, Jingsen Zhang, Zhiyuan Chen, Jiakai Tang, Xu Chen, Yankai Lin, Wayne Xin Zhao, Zhewei Wei, and Ji-Rong Wen. 2024c. A survey on large language model based autonomous agents. *Front. Comput. Sci.*, 18.

Lei Wang, Wanyu Xu, Yihuai Lan, Zhiqiang Hu, Yunshi Lan, Roy Ka-Wei Lee, and Ee-Peng Lim. 2023d. Plan-and-solve prompting: Improving zero-shot chain-of-thought reasoning by large language models. In *ACL (1)*, pages 2609–2634. Association for Computational Linguistics.

Peifeng Wang, Zhengyang Wang, Zheng Li, Yifan Gao, Bing Yin, and Xiang Ren. 2023e. SCOTT: self-consistent chain-of-thought distillation. In *ACL (1)*, pages 5546–5558. Association for Computational Linguistics.

Xuezhi Wang, Jason Wei, Dale Schuurmans, Quoc V Le, Ed H. Chi, Sharan Narang, Aakanksha Chowdhery, and Denny Zhou. 2023f. Self-consistency improves chain of thought reasoning in language models. In *The Eleventh International Conference on Learning Representations*.

Yiming Wang, Zhuosheng Zhang, Pei Zhang, Baosong Yang, and Rui Wang. 2024d. Meta-reasoning: Semantics-symbol deconstruction for large language models. In *ACL (Findings)*. Association for Computational Linguistics.

Zekun Wang, Ge Zhang, Kexin Yang, Ning Shi, Wangchunshu Zhou, Shaochun Hao, Guangzheng Xiong, Yizhi Li, Mong Yuan Sim, Xiuying Chen, Qingqing Zhu, Zhenzhu Yang, Adam Nik, Qi Liu, Chenghua Lin, Shi Wang, Ruibo Liu, Wenhu Chen, Ke Xu, Dayiheng Liu, Yike Guo, and Jie Fu. 2023g. Interactive natural language processing. *CoRR*, abs/2305.13246.

Zhaoyang Wang, Shaohan Huang, Yuxuan Liu, Jiahai Wang, Minghui Song, Zihan Zhang, Haizhen Huang, Furu Wei, Weiwei Deng, Feng Sun, and Qi Zhang. 2023h. Democratizing reasoning ability: Tailored learning from large language model. In *EMNLP*, pages 1948–1966. Association for Computational Linguistics.

Jason Wei, Xuezhi Wang, Dale Schuurmans, Maarten Bosma, Brian Ichter, Fei Xia, Ed H. Chi, Quoc V. Le, and Denny Zhou. 2022. Chain-of-thought prompting elicits reasoning in large language models. In *NeurIPS*.

Yixuan Weng, Minjun Zhu, Fei Xia, Bin Li, Shizhu He, Shengping Liu, Bin Sun, Kang Liu, and Jun Zhao. 2023. Large language models are better reasoners with self-verification. In *EMNLP (Findings)*, pages 2550–2575. Association for Computational Linguistics.

Zhenyu Wu, Meng Jiang, and Chao Shen. 2024. Get an a in math: Progressive rectification prompting. In *AAAI*. AAAI Press.

Zhiheng Xi, Wenxiang Chen, Xin Guo, Wei He, Yiwen Ding, Boyang Hong, Ming Zhang, Junzhe Wang, Senjie Jin, Enyu Zhou, Rui Zheng, Xiaoran Fan, Xiao Wang, Limao Xiong, Yuhao Zhou, Weiran Wang, Changhao Jiang, Yicheng Zou, Xiangyang Liu, Zhangyue Yin, Shihan Dou, Rongxiang Weng, Wensen Cheng, Qi Zhang, Wenjuan Qin, Yongyan Zheng, Xipeng Qiu, Xuanjing Huan, and Tao Gui. 2023a. The rise and potential of large language model based agents: A survey. *CoRR*, abs/2309.07864.

Zhiheng Xi, Senjie Jin, Yuhao Zhou, Rui Zheng, Songyang Gao, Jia Liu, Tao Gui, Qi Zhang, and Xuanjing Huang. 2023b. Self-polish: Enhance reasoning in large language models via problem refinement. In *EMNLP (Findings)*, pages 11383–11406. Association for Computational Linguistics.

Miao Xiong, Zhiyuan Hu, Xinyang Lu, Yifei Li, Jie Fu, Junxian He, and Bryan Hooi. 2024. Can llms express their uncertainty? an empirical evaluation of confidence elicitation in llms. In *ICLR*. OpenReview.net.

Xiaohan Xu, Chongyang Tao, Tao Shen, Can Xu, Hongbo Xu, Guodong Long, and Jianguang Lou. 2023. Re-reading improves reasoning in language models. *CoRR*, abs/2309.06275.

Tianci Xue, Ziqi Wang, Zhenhailong Wang, Chi Han, Pengfei Yu, and Heng Ji. 2023. RCOT: detecting and rectifying factual inconsistency in reasoning by reversing chain-of-thought. *CoRR*, abs/2305.11499.

Fanglong Yao, Changyuan Tian, Jintao Liu, Zequn Zhang, Qing Liu, Li Jin, Shuchao Li, Xiaoyu Li, and Xian Sun. 2023a. Thinking like an expert: Multimodal hypergraph-of-thought (hot) reasoning to boost foundation modals. *CoRR*, abs/2308.06207.

Shunyu Yao, Dian Yu, Jeffrey Zhao, Izhak Shafran, Thomas L. Griffiths, Yuan Cao, and Karthik Narasimhan. 2023b. Tree of thoughts: Deliberate problem solving with large language models. In *NeurIPS*.

Shunyu Yao, Jeffrey Zhao, Dian Yu, Nan Du, Izhak Shafran, Karthik R. Narasimhan, and Yuan Cao. 2023c. React: Synergizing reasoning and acting in language models. In *ICLR*. OpenReview.net.

Weiran Yao, Shelby Heinecke, Juan Carlos Niebles, Zhiwei Liu, Yihao Feng, Le Xue, Rithesh Murthy, Zeyuan Chen, Jianguo Zhang, Devansh Arpit, Ran Xu, Phil Mui, Huan Wang, Caiming Xiong, and Silvio Savarese. 2024. Retroformer: Retrospective large language agents with policy gradient optimization. In *ICLR*. OpenReview.net.

Yao Yao, Zuchao Li, and Hai Zhao. 2023d. Beyond chain-of-thought, effective graph-of-thought reasoning in large language models. *CoRR*, abs/2305.16582.

Ori Yoran, Tomer Wolfson, Ben Bogin, Uri Katz, Daniel Deutch, and Jonathan Berant. 2023. Answering questions by meta-reasoning over multiple chains of thought. In *EMNLP*, pages 5942–5966. Association for Computational Linguistics.

Xiang Yue, Xingwei Qu, Ge Zhang, Yao Fu, Wenhao Huang, Huan Sun, Yu Su, and Wenhu Chen. 2024. Mammoth: Building math generalist models through hybrid instruction tuning. In *ICLR*. OpenReview.net.

Eric Zelikman, Yuhuai Wu, Jesse Mu, and Noah Goodman. 2022. STar: Bootstrapping reasoning with reasoning. In *NeurIPS*.

Mengxue Zhang, Zichao Wang, Zhichao Yang, Weiqi Feng, and Andrew S. Lan. 2023. Interpretable math word problem solution generation via step-by-step planning. In *ACL (1)*, pages 6858–6877. Association for Computational Linguistics.

Ruochen Zhao, Xingxuan Li, Shafiq R. Joty, Chengwei Qin, and Lidong Bing. 2023a. Verify-and-edit: A knowledge-enhanced chain-of-thought framework. In *ACL (1)*, pages 5823–5840. Association for Computational Linguistics.

Wayne Xin Zhao, Kun Zhou, Junyi Li, Tianyi Tang, Xiaolei Wang, Yupeng Hou, Yingqian Min, Beichen Zhang, Junjie Zhang, Zican Dong, Yifan Du, Chen Yang, Yushuo Chen, Zhipeng Chen, Jinhao Jiang, Ruiyang Ren, Yifan Li, Xinyu Tang, Zikang Liu, Peiyu Liu, Jian-Yun Nie, and Ji-Rong Wen. 2023b. A survey of large language models. *CoRR*, abs/2303.18223.

Chuanyang Zheng, Zhengying Liu, Enze Xie, Zhenguo Li, and Yu Li. 2023. Progressive-hint prompting improves reasoning in large language models. *CoRR*, abs/2304.09797.

Aojun Zhou, Ke Wang, Zimu Lu, Weikang Shi, Sichun Luo, Zipeng Qin, Shaoqing Lu, Anya Jia, Linqi Song, Mingjie Zhan, and Hongsheng Li. 2024. Solving challenging math word problems using GPT-4 code interpreter with code-based self-verification. In *ICLR*. OpenReview.net.

Appendices

A Terminology Clarification of Answer Calibration and Model Calibration

To avoid the confusion caused by the usage of the already-existing concept *"calibration"*, we provide a terminology clarification. We emphasize that ***"answer calibration"* defined in our paper differs from *"model calibration"*** (Niculescu-Mizil and Caruana, 2005; Guo et al., 2017; Tian et al., 2023; Xiong et al., 2024). *"Answer Calibration"* refers to the post-processing methods applied to one or more reasoning path(s), to obtain a final answer. We categorize answer calibration methods as 'step-level' if they break down the reasoning path(s) into their individual steps, and 'path-level' otherwise. In most cases, *"Answer Calibration"* is more akin to *"Answer Correction"* (Pan et al., 2024), involves correcting mistakes in the initial output. We did give a definition like this in the *Abstract*, *Introduction*, and we have already provided clear definitions of *"Answer Calibration"* in §3.

B Model Choice Justification

The choice of GPT-3.5 was driven by its relevance and accessibility for our research objectives. Our research includes an empirical study of answer calibration and a proposal of a unified method, where the backbone LLM is pluggable. To facilitate reproducibility, we have already released the code and LLM-generated data anonymously[1] (provided at the bottom of Page 5 in §4), aiming to enhance transparency to some extent and facilitate further research in this area. We remain committed to exploring more transparent models in future work.

C Cases of Low-Quality Prompts

We list some examples of prompts in Table 3.

Prompt Setting	***Example Query (Arithmetic Reasoning)*** *Leah had 32 chocolates and her sister had 42.* *If they ate 35,* *how many pieces do they have left in total?*
Standard CoT	Originally, Leah had 32 chocolates and her sister had 42. So in total they had 32 + 42 = 74. After eating 35, they had 74 - 35 = 39 pieces left in total. The answer is 39.
No Coherence	After eating 32 + 42 = 74, they had 32 pieces left in total. Originally, Leah had 74 - 35 = 39 chocolates and her sister had 35. So in total they had 42. The answer is 39.
No Relevance	Patricia needs to donate 19 inches, and wants her hair to be 31 inches long after the donation. Her hair is 29 inches long currently. Her hair needs to be 19 + 31 = 50 inc long when she cuts it. So she needs to grow 50 - 29 = 21 more inches. The answer is 21.

Table 3: Examples of prompts (standard, no coherence and no relevance) in our experiments.

Applying RLAIF for Code Generation with API-usage in Lightweight LLMs

Sujan Dutta[1,†], Sayantan Mahinder[2], Raviteja Anantha[2], and Bortik Bandyopadhyay[2]

[1]Rochester Institute of Technology, sd2516@rit.edu
[2]Apple, {smahinder, raviteja_anantha, bbandyopadhyay}@apple.com

Abstract

Reinforcement Learning from AI Feedback (RLAIF) has demonstrated significant potential across various domains, including mitigating harm in LLM outputs, enhancing text summarization, and mathematical reasoning. This paper introduces an RLAIF framework for improving the code generation abilities of lightweight (<1B parameters) LLMs. We specifically focus on code generation tasks that require writing appropriate API calls, which is challenging due to the well-known issue of hallucination in LLMs. Our framework extracts AI feedback from a larger LLM (e.g., GPT-3.5) through a specialized prompting strategy and uses this data to train a reward model towards better alignment from smaller LLMs. We run our experiments on the Gorilla dataset and meticulously assess the quality of the model-generated code across various metrics, including AST, ROUGE, and Code-BLEU, and develop a pipeline to compute its executability rate accurately. Our approach significantly enhances the fine-tuned LLM baseline's performance, achieving a 4.5% improvement in executability rate. Notably, a smaller LLM model (780M parameters) trained with RLAIF surpasses a much larger fine-tuned baseline with 7B parameters, achieving a 1.0% higher code executability rate.

1 Introduction

LLMs have demonstrated unprecedented natural language understanding and generation capabilities in recent times (Brown et al., 2020; Chowdhery et al., 2022; OpenAI, 2023; Anil et al., 2023; Jiang et al., 2023; Touvron et al., 2023). Reinforcement Learning with Human Feedback (RLHF) is a key contributor to this success. RLHF is a fine-tuning approach that uses human feedback to train models by incorporating human evaluations into the reward signal. This method improves model performance on complex tasks by aligning the model's behavior with human preferences. However, this technique is expensive due to the requirement for high-quality human feedback. RLAIF (Bai et al., 2022; Lee et al., 2023) has emerged as a promising alternative to replace human feedback with AI feedback, making the fine-tuning more scalable. Concurrently, there is growing research interest in teaching LLMs how to use external tools (APIs) (Schick et al., 2024; Nakano et al., 2021; Patil et al., 2023; Qin et al., 2023; Li et al., 2023; Zhuang et al., 2024; Hao et al., 2024). However, the focus on lightweight models (<1B parameters) is limited. In this work, we propose an RLAIF framework to enhance lightweight LLMs' capability to generate code and effectively integrate API calls. Following Patil *et al.* (2023), we consider the task of generating Python codes that include suitable API calls given instructions across a wide array of applications. The authors published the Gorilla dataset and showed that fine-tuned `LLaMA-7B` (Touvron et al., 2023) on this dataset outperforms non-finetuned LLMs like `GPT-4` (OpenAI, 2023) in terms of understanding a natural language request and mapping it to API calls. Using our RLAIF framework, we fine-tune `GPT-2-large` (Radford et al., 2019) (780M parameters), which not only demonstrates comparable API call correctness to (Patil et al., 2023) but also surpasses its code generation performance.

Code Generation. Although extensively studied since the early days of AI research, code generation (Waldinger and Lee, 1969; Budinsky et al., 1996; Svyatkovskiy et al., 2020; Li et al., 2022) remains a challenging problem. In recent years, the community has explored ways to apply RL in training machine learning models for code generation tasks. For instance, *Seq2SQL* (Zhong et al., 2017) proposed a neural network trained through RL for generating SQL queries given a text description. During training, a generated query is executed

† Work done as a part of an internship at Apple.

Proceedings of the 2nd Workshop on Natural Language Reasoning and Structured Explanations (@ACL 2024), pages 39–45
August 15, 2024 ©2024 Association for Computational Linguistics

against a database, and the result is utilized as the reward in the RL algorithm. Le *et al.* (2022) developed *CodeRL*, a sequence-to-sequence language model fine-tuned through an actor-critic RL approach for program synthesis. The code-generator LM is treated as the actor during the training, and the critic model, which is trained to predict unit test results, provides the reward for a generated code. Another work (Shojaee et al., 2023) similar to the above, proposed using feedback from code execution and a ground truth target code to compute the reward. While these approaches may perform well on classical programming tasks (e.g., writing SQL queries, solving competitive/interview-level coding problems, etc.), they are inapplicable on Gorilla-like (Patil et al., 2023) code generation where the program is required to load and execute ML models using the correct API. The bottleneck comes from the fact that the above-mentioned techniques require execution of the generated code to either compute the reward directly or train the critic model, but running thousands of such programs is prohibitively expensive.

Reinforcement Learning with AI Feedback. Bai *et al.* (2022) introduced the concept of Reinforcement Learning with AI Feedback (RLAIF), which combines preferences labeled by LLMs with human-labeled preferences to optimize for helpfulness and harmlessness. Since then, many studies have explored the usefulness of AI-generated feedback as an alternative to expensive human annotations in various tasks. For instance, Luo *et al.* (2023) proposed *WizardMath*, which enhances the mathematical reasoning abilities of `Llama-2` using AI feedback in the training process. In another work (Zhang et al., 2023), researchers used real-world data along with RLAIF to improve LLMs as medical consultants. Prior research has also explored AI evaluation for improving factual correctness in LLM-generated medical summaries (Mishra et al., 2023). Kwon *et al.* (2023) explored the usefulness of LLMs in the reward design for RL agents in Ultimatum Game, matrix games, and the DealOrNoDeal negotiation task. Recently, Lee *et al.* (2023) demonstrated that RLAIF can achieve human-level performance in summarization and helpful and harmless text generation. However, the possibility of using RLAIF to improve the code generation and API usage ability in small models (<1B parameters) is under-explored. We demonstrate that even with a few model parameters, AI feedback significantly improves code generation quality over simple fine-tuning baselines. Moreover, we found RLAIF applied on smaller 780M parameter `GPT-2-large` model outperforms `LLaMA-7B` fine-tuned models, which has nine times more parameters.

2 Dataset

We applied our proposed method to the Gorilla dataset published by Patil *et al.* (2023). The Gorilla dataset consists of three parts - HuggingFace, TensorFlow, and PyTorch. In this work, we only focus on the HuggingFace dataset, which is the most extensive among the three, featuring over 925 unique APIs. These APIs belong to 37 different domains (e.g., Multimodal Text-to-Image, Computer Vision Image Classification, Audio Text-to-Speech, etc.), and for each API, there exist ten unique instructions. Each instance of the data contains an *instruction* (task description), *domain*, *API call* (a single code line), *explanation* (how to solve the task using the API), and a complete *code* (Python script) to accomplish the task. Here, we highlight some key differences between Gorilla and the traditional code generation datasets. Most of the problem statements and corresponding code snippets present in the benchmark datasets including CodeSearchNet (Husain et al., 2019), XLCoST (Zhu et al., 2022), APPS (Hendrycks et al., 2021) and MBPP (Austin et al., 2021) are related to traditional software engineering tasks, representative of common interview questions, require minimal computational resources to execute and do not require internet connection. On the contrary, the Python scripts in the Gorilla dataset focus on AI-related tasks and require an internet connection and significant computing resources (storage and processing power) to execute. The scripts are expected to download ML models hosted on HuggingFace, load them in memory, and run inference. So, techniques where code execution or unit test outcomes are treated as feedback (Zhong et al., 2017; Le et al., 2022; Shojaee et al., 2023) become inapplicable.

While Patil *et al.* (2023) focused only on generating the API call, we demonstrate the effectiveness of our approach both on API call correctness and the ability to use that API in a complete code.

3 Methodology

Our framework follows a similar pipeline to RLHF (Ouyang et al., 2022). However, instead of asking

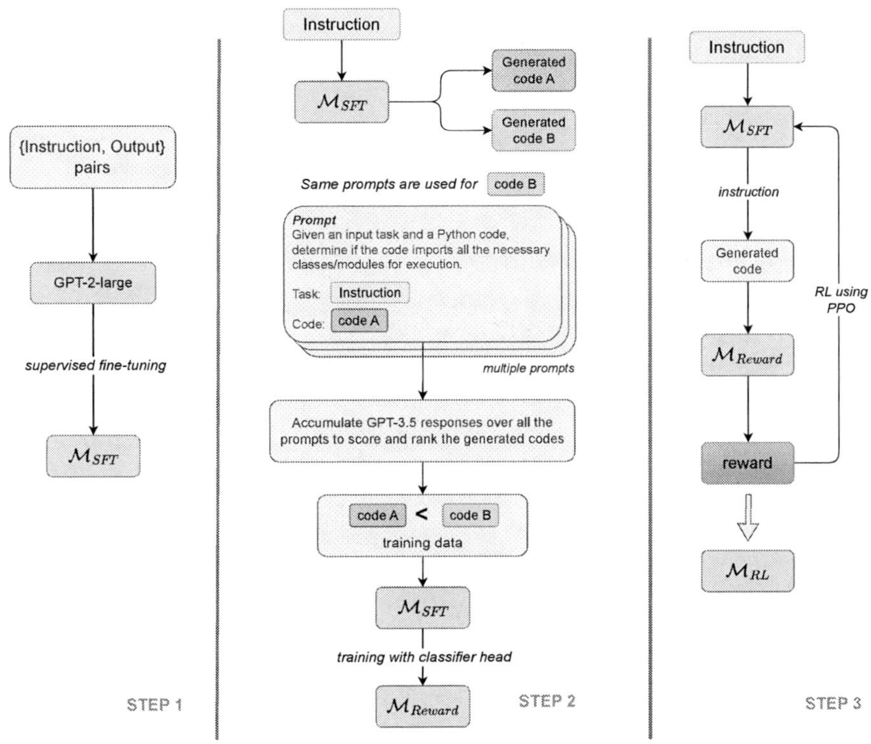

Figure 1: Schematic diagram of the proposed framework. Step 1 is to fine-tune a base model on the dataset. In step 2, we score the $\mathcal{M}_{SFT}$ generated outputs based on the `GPT-3.5` feedback using the technique described in section 3. Using this score, we prepare preference data and train a reward model. Finally, in step 3, we use RL to fine-tune $\mathcal{M}_{SFT}$ where $\mathcal{M}_{reward}$ provides the reward.

human annotators to rank the generated responses, we employ a bigger LLM by using a novel prompting strategy. More specifically, for a given instruction and generated code (containing an API call), we ask multiple binary (*yes/no*) questions that capture different aspects of the generated code (and API call) to determine its quality. Our intuition is, that while generating code from natural language might be still challenging for LLMs, providing binary (*yes/no*) answers guided by few-shot exemplars is a much easier task. These feedbacks in turn could be aggregated as a preference ground truth to train the reward model in the RLHF (Ouyang et al., 2022) process. Thus our approach eliminates the need for expensive human annotation cost. We describe the proposed framework (Figure 1) in detail.

- ***Step 1: Training a base model***

The first step in the pipeline is to fine-tune a language model on the dataset to get a base model. We choose `GPT-2-large` and train it on the Gorilla dataset using the supervised fine-tuning technique for causal language models. We denote the fine-tuned model by $\mathcal{M}_{SFT}$.

- ***Step 2: Training a reward model using LLM feedback***

Instead of human feedback from annotators, we employed a bigger LLM to generate the labels for the reward model. We realized that human graders while judging the correctness of a response, consider different aspects of the generated output. Based on this intuition, we created multiple prompts (P_i) that ask different questions (Q_i) for the same input-output pair. More specifically, we created a set of 8 questions which We feed as prompts to a state-of-the-art language model (GPT-3.5) to get a binary response. Each of these questions addresses a different desired quality (free of bugs, correct imports, no undefined variables, correct syntax, etc.) of the output relevant to the task. Step 2 in Figure 1 presents a sample prompt made using one of the questions. The appendix contains the complete list of prompts. As the questions are binary (*yes/no*) in nature, we simply count the number of *yes* replies by $\mathcal{M}_{GPT\,3.5}$ to score each input-output pair. More formally, given a task t, generated output o, and question set $\{Q_i\}$ the prompt set is defined as $P(t,o) = \{P_i \mid P_i = [Q_i, t, o]\}$. The corresponding score (S) is given as:

$$S(t,o) = \frac{\sum_{P_i \in P(t,o)} \mathbb{I}(\mathcal{M}_{GPT\,3.5}(P_i) = yes)}{|P(t,o)|}$$

where $\mathbb{I}$ is the indicator function and $\mathcal{M}_{GPT\,3.5}(P_i)$ is the reply from $\mathcal{M}_{GPT\,3.5}$ for the prompt P_i. We use this score to prepare the training data for $\mathcal{M}_{reward}$ in the following way. For each instruction in the training data, we generate two outputs from $\mathcal{M}_{SFT}$ by varying the generation parameters (top-k, temperature, etc.). Then they are scored using the method described above and labeled (accept or reject) based on this score. These tuples of {*input instruction, accepted output, rejected output*} are then combined to form the dataset for $\mathcal{M}_{reward}$. In the training phase, $\mathcal{M}_{reward}$ learns to classify whether a machine-generated code is acceptable (or not) for a given input instruction. We append a classifier head on top of $\mathcal{M}_{SFT}$ and use this as the starting point of $\mathcal{M}_{reward}$ and train for three epochs.

- ***Step 3: Reinforcement Learning***

Finally, in the RL step, we fine-tune $\mathcal{M}_{SFT}$ using the proximal policy optimization (PPO) algorithm (Schulman et al., 2017). The reward in this step is given by $\mathcal{M}_{reward}$'s logit scores. We denote our final fine-tuned model by $\mathcal{M}_{RL}$.

4 Results and Discussions

Model Name (Size)	Executability Rate (%)	ROUGE (×100)	CodeBLEU (×100)	AST (%)
$\mathcal{M}_{Gorilla}$ (2023) (7B)	26.9	41.2	36.8	71.68
$\mathcal{M}_{SFT}$ (780M)	23.4	47.2	40.6	72.96
$\mathcal{M}_{RL}$ (780M)	**27.9**	**47.5**	**42.2**	**73.62**

Table 1: Performance comparison of different models on the Gorilla dataset.

We compute the code generation quality using multiple metrics by comparing the generated output with the ground truth. The reported *ROUGE* is the average of *ROUGE-1, ROUGE-2, ROUGE-L, and ROUGE-sum* metrics introduced in (Lin, 2004). *CodeBLEU* (Ren et al., 2020) was specifically designed for evaluating code synthesis. Ren *et al.* (2020) defined *CodeBLEU* as the weighted average of standard *BLEU* (Papineni et al., 2002), the weighted n-gram match ($BLEU_{weight}$), the syntactic AST match ($Match_{ast}$), and the semantic dataflow match ($Match_{df}$). $CodeBLEU = \alpha \cdot BLEU + \beta \cdot BLEU_{weight} + \gamma \cdot Match_{ast} + \delta \cdot Match_{df}$. We set $\alpha = \beta = \gamma = \delta = 0.25$ to give equal importance to all the components. The AST sub-tree-matching metric was proposed in (Patil et al., 2023) to capture the correctness of the API calls. In addition to that, we also report the successful execution rate of the generated code (*Executability Rate*). It is worth noting that running this amount of machine-generated programs that download and use large AI models is challenging. We created a pipeline to automatically run the machine-generated codes in an isolated environment.

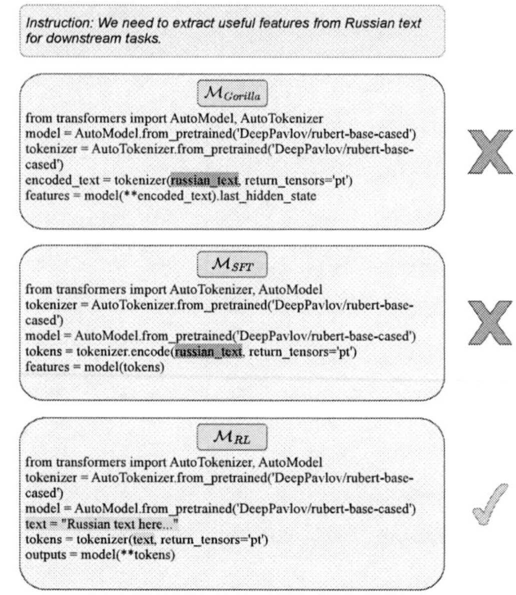

Figure 2: Example code generated by different models for the same instruction. In the generations of $\mathcal{M}_{Gorilla}$ and $\mathcal{M}_{SFT}$ the variable `russian_text` is undefined and hence will result in an error. Whereas $\mathcal{M}_{RL}$ defines the variable `text` before using it.

Table 1 compares the performance of the proposed model with $\mathcal{M}_{Gorilla}$ (finetuned `LLaMA-7B`) (2023). The results clearly show that the proposed $\mathcal{M}_{RL}$ boosts the performance of the supervised fine-tuned $\mathcal{M}_{SFT}$ in terms of *CodeBLEU* (1.6 points abs), *AST* (0.66% abs) and *Executability Rate* (4.5% abs). We also note that $\mathcal{M}_{RL}$ outperforms the $\mathcal{M}_{Gorilla}$ despite having only 1/9-th of the parameters. It is also reflected in the *Executability Rate* of the generated code. Figure 2 shows an instance where our framework helps in fixing a common error present in $\mathcal{M}_{Gorilla}$ and $\mathcal{M}_{SFT}$ generations.

5 Ethics statement

This work adheres to the ethical guidelines and principles set out in the ACM Code of Ethics and followed by the broader research community. The dataset used in this paper was originally collected from public repositories hosted on HuggingFace. The authors are aware of the growing literature on jailbreaking language models to generate unsafe content. We hope the community will use the proposed models responsibly and only for the intended use cases.

6 Limitations

One of the common limitations faced by similar fine-tuned models is the presence of biases inherited from the pre-trained model. We anticipate that the biases present in the chosen base model (`GPT-2-large`) also exist in the final model $\mathcal{M}_{RL}$ which might lead to the generation of biased code comments.

Another limitation of this work is the lack of diversity in programming language. The public dataset we considered contains only Python code. Future work should consider expanding this approach to encompass additional programming languages such as C++, Java, JavaScript, etc. Besides, we have not analyzed the performance between more frequent APIs (head) and infrequent APIs (tail). There might be some scope for improvements by focusing on tail APIs more.

Lastly, the learning methodology applied in this study is offline. Given the rapid evolution and proliferation of machine learning models and the corresponding APIs for specific tasks, the model may not leverage more suitable APIs that emerge post-training. To address this, periodic updates to the model are necessary. Our framework's reliance on machine-generated feedback significantly reduces the resource intensity associated with the RLHF process, making these updates more feasible and less costly than a human feedback-based approach.

References

Rohan Anil, Andrew M Dai, Orhan Firat, Melvin Johnson, Dmitry Lepikhin, Alexandre Passos, Siamak Shakeri, Emanuel Taropa, Paige Bailey, Zhifeng Chen, et al. 2023. Palm 2 technical report. *arXiv preprint arXiv:2305.10403*.

Jacob Austin, Augustus Odena, Maxwell Nye, Maarten Bosma, Henryk Michalewski, David Dohan, Ellen Jiang, Carrie Cai, Michael Terry, Quoc Le, et al. 2021. Program synthesis with large language models. *arXiv preprint arXiv:2108.07732*.

Yuntao Bai, Saurav Kadavath, Sandipan Kundu, Amanda Askell, Jackson Kernion, Andy Jones, Anna Chen, Anna Goldie, Azalia Mirhoseini, Cameron McKinnon, et al. 2022. Constitutional ai: Harmlessness from ai feedback. *arXiv preprint arXiv:2212.08073*.

Tom Brown, Benjamin Mann, Nick Ryder, Melanie Subbiah, Jared D Kaplan, Prafulla Dhariwal, Arvind Neelakantan, Pranav Shyam, Girish Sastry, Amanda Askell, et al. 2020. Language models are few-shot learners. *Advances in neural information processing systems*, 33:1877–1901.

Frank J. Budinsky, Marilyn A. Finnie, John M. Vlissides, and Patsy S. Yu. 1996. Automatic code generation from design patterns. *IBM systems Journal*, 35(2):151–171.

Aakanksha Chowdhery, Sharan Narang, Jacob Devlin, Maarten Bosma, Gaurav Mishra, Adam Roberts, Paul Barham, Hyung Won Chung, Charles Sutton, Sebastian Gehrmann, et al. 2022. Palm: Scaling language modeling with pathways. *arXiv preprint arXiv:2204.02311*.

Shibo Hao, Tianyang Liu, Zhen Wang, and Zhiting Hu. 2024. Toolkengpt: Augmenting frozen language models with massive tools via tool embeddings. *Advances in neural information processing systems*, 36.

Dan Hendrycks, Steven Basart, Saurav Kadavath, Mantas Mazeika, Akul Arora, Ethan Guo, Collin Burns, Samir Puranik, Horace He, Dawn Song, and Jacob Steinhardt. 2021. Measuring coding challenge competence with apps. *NeurIPS*.

Hamel Husain, Ho-Hsiang Wu, Tiferet Gazit, Miltiadis Allamanis, and Marc Brockschmidt. 2019. CodeSearchNet challenge: Evaluating the state of semantic code search. *arXiv preprint arXiv:1909.09436*.

Albert Q Jiang, Alexandre Sablayrolles, Arthur Mensch, Chris Bamford, Devendra Singh Chaplot, Diego de las Casas, Florian Bressand, Gianna Lengyel, Guillaume Lample, Lucile Saulnier, et al. 2023. Mistral 7b. *arXiv preprint arXiv:2310.06825*.

Minae Kwon, Sang Michael Xie, Kalesha Bullard, and Dorsa Sadigh. 2023. Reward design with language models. *arXiv preprint arXiv:2303.00001*.

Hung Le, Yue Wang, Akhilesh Deepak Gotmare, Silvio Savarese, and Steven Chu Hong Hoi. 2022. Coderl: Mastering code generation through pretrained models and deep reinforcement learning. *Advances in Neural Information Processing Systems*, 35:21314–21328.

Harrison Lee, Samrat Phatale, Hassan Mansoor, Kellie Lu, Thomas Mesnard, Colton Bishop, Victor Carbune, and Abhinav Rastogi. 2023. Rlaif: Scaling reinforcement learning from human feedback with ai feedback. *arXiv preprint arXiv:2309.00267*.

Minghao Li, Feifan Song, Bowen Yu, Haiyang Yu, Zhoujun Li, Fei Huang, and Yongbin Li. 2023. Api-bank: A benchmark for tool-augmented llms. *arXiv preprint arXiv:2304.08244*.

Yujia Li, David Choi, Junyoung Chung, Nate Kushman, Julian Schrittwieser, Rémi Leblond, Tom Eccles, James Keeling, Felix Gimeno, Agustin Dal Lago, et al. 2022. Competition-level code generation with alphacode. *Science*, 378(6624):1092–1097.

Chin-Yew Lin. 2004. Rouge: A package for automatic evaluation of summaries. In *Text summarization branches out*, pages 74–81.

Haipeng Luo, Qingfeng Sun, Can Xu, Pu Zhao, Jianguang Lou, Chongyang Tao, Xiubo Geng, Qingwei Lin, Shifeng Chen, and Dongmei Zhang. 2023. Wizardmath: Empowering mathematical reasoning for large language models via reinforced evol-instruct. *arXiv preprint arXiv:2308.09583*.

Prakamya Mishra, Zonghai Yao, Shuwei Chen, Beining Wang, Rohan Mittal, and Hong Yu. 2023. Synthetic imitation edit feedback for factual alignment in clinical summarization. *arXiv preprint arXiv:2310.20033*.

Reiichiro Nakano, Jacob Hilton, Suchir Balaji, Jeff Wu, Long Ouyang, Christina Kim, Christopher Hesse, Shantanu Jain, Vineet Kosaraju, William Saunders, et al. 2021. Webgpt: Browser-assisted question-answering with human feedback. *arXiv preprint arXiv:2112.09332*.

OpenAI. 2023. Gpt-4 technical report.

Long Ouyang, Jeffrey Wu, Xu Jiang, Diogo Almeida, Carroll Wainwright, Pamela Mishkin, Chong Zhang, Sandhini Agarwal, Katarina Slama, Alex Ray, et al. 2022. Training language models to follow instructions with human feedback. *Advances in Neural Information Processing Systems*, 35:27730–27744.

Kishore Papineni, Salim Roukos, Todd Ward, and Wei-Jing Zhu. 2002. Bleu: a method for automatic evaluation of machine translation. In *Proceedings of the 40th annual meeting of the Association for Computational Linguistics*, pages 311–318.

Shishir G. Patil, Tianjun Zhang, Xin Wang, and Joseph E. Gonzalez. 2023. Gorilla: Large language model connected with massive apis. *arXiv preprint arXiv:2305.15334*.

Yujia Qin, Shihao Liang, Yining Ye, Kunlun Zhu, Lan Yan, Yaxi Lu, Yankai Lin, Xin Cong, Xiangru Tang, Bill Qian, et al. 2023. Toolllm: Facilitating large language models to master 16000+ real-world apis. *arXiv preprint arXiv:2307.16789*.

Alec Radford, Jeffrey Wu, Rewon Child, David Luan, Dario Amodei, Ilya Sutskever, et al. 2019. Language models are unsupervised multitask learners. *OpenAI blog*, 1(8):9.

Shuo Ren, Daya Guo, Shuai Lu, Long Zhou, Shujie Liu, Duyu Tang, Neel Sundaresan, Ming Zhou, Ambrosio Blanco, and Shuai Ma. 2020. Codebleu: a method for automatic evaluation of code synthesis. *arXiv preprint arXiv:2009.10297*.

Timo Schick, Jane Dwivedi-Yu, Roberto Dessì, Roberta Raileanu, Maria Lomeli, Eric Hambro, Luke Zettlemoyer, Nicola Cancedda, and Thomas Scialom. 2024. Toolformer: Language models can teach themselves to use tools. *Advances in Neural Information Processing Systems*, 36.

John Schulman, Filip Wolski, Prafulla Dhariwal, Alec Radford, and Oleg Klimov. 2017. Proximal policy optimization algorithms. *arXiv preprint arXiv:1707.06347*.

Parshin Shojaee, Aneesh Jain, Sindhu Tipirneni, and Chandan K Reddy. 2023. Execution-based code generation using deep reinforcement learning. *arXiv preprint arXiv:2301.13816*.

Alexey Svyatkovskiy, Shao Kun Deng, Shengyu Fu, and Neel Sundaresan. 2020. Intellicode compose: Code generation using transformer. In *Proceedings of the 28th ACM Joint Meeting on European Software Engineering Conference and Symposium on the Foundations of Software Engineering*, pages 1433–1443.

Hugo Touvron, Thibaut Lavril, Gautier Izacard, Xavier Martinet, Marie-Anne Lachaux, Timothée Lacroix, Baptiste Rozière, Naman Goyal, Eric Hambro, Faisal Azhar, et al. 2023. Llama: Open and efficient foundation language models. *arXiv preprint arXiv:2302.13971*.

Leandro von Werra, Younes Belkada, Lewis Tunstall, Edward Beeching, Tristan Thrush, Nathan Lambert, and Shengyi Huang. 2020. Trl: Transformer reinforcement learning. `https://github.com/huggingface/trl`.

Richard J Waldinger and Richard CT Lee. 1969. Prow: A step toward automatic program writing. In *Proceedings of the 1st international joint conference on Artificial intelligence*, pages 241–252.

Thomas Wolf, Lysandre Debut, Victor Sanh, Julien Chaumond, Clement Delangue, Anthony Moi, Pierric Cistac, Tim Rault, Rémi Louf, Morgan Funtowicz, et al. 2020. Transformers: State-of-the-art natural language processing. In *Proceedings of the 2020 conference on empirical methods in natural language processing: system demonstrations*, pages 38–45.

Hongbo Zhang, Junying Chen, Feng Jiang, Fei Yu, Zhihong Chen, Jianquan Li, Guiming Chen, Xiangbo Wu, Zhiyi Zhang, Qingying Xiao, et al. 2023. Huatuogpt, towards taming language model to be a doctor. *arXiv preprint arXiv:2305.15075*.

Victor Zhong, Caiming Xiong, and Richard Socher. 2017. Seq2sql: Generating structured queries from natural language using reinforcement learning. *arXiv preprint arXiv:1709.00103*.

Ming Zhu, Aneesh Jain, Karthik Suresh, Roshan Ravindran, Sindhu Tipirneni, and Chandan K. Reddy. 2022. Xlcost: A benchmark dataset for cross-lingual code intelligence.

Yuchen Zhuang, Yue Yu, Kuan Wang, Haotian Sun, and Chao Zhang. 2024. Toolqa: A dataset for llm question answering with external tools. *Advances in Neural Information Processing Systems*, 36.

A Prompts

Table 2 lists all the prompts used in accessing the quality of the generated codes.

B Experimental details

B.1 Dataset

The HuggingFace part of the Gorilla dataset (Patil et al., 2023) consists of over 9k instruction-output pairs. We trained our model on 90% of the data and kept the rest for evaluation.

B.2 Model and implementation details

$\mathcal{M}_{SFT}$, $\mathcal{M}_{reward}$ and $\mathcal{M}_{RL}$ all have 780M parameters. While training $\mathcal{M}_{SFT}$ and $\mathcal{M}_{reward}$ we used a learning rate of 5×10^{-4} and 5×10^{-5} respectively. In the RL step (PPO algorithm), we set the learning rate to 6×10^{-6}. We did not perform any hyperparameter search. The results are reported by taking the mean of three inference runs. We implemented the training pipeline using the following Python libraries: transformers (Wolf et al., 2020) and TRL (von Werra et al., 2020).

B.3 Computational cost

We used a cluster of NVIDIA A100 40GB GPUs for our experiments. We spent in total $\sim$ 60 GPU hours for all of the experiments.

Prompt

`Given an input task and a Python code, determine if the code is functional.`
`TASK: [instruction]`
`CODE: [code]`

`Given an input task and a Python code, determine if the code imports all the necessary classes/modules for execution.`
`TASK: [instruction]`
`CODE: [code]`

`Given an input task and a Python code, determine if the code uses the correct functions/APIs.`
`TASK: [instruction]`
`CODE: [code]`

`Given an input task and a Python code, determine if the code is free of bugs and code smells.`
`TASK: [instruction]`
`CODE: [code]`

`Given an input task and a Python code, determine if the code is sufficient to accomplish the task.`
`TASK: [instruction]`
`CODE: [code]`

`Given an input task and a Python code, determine if the code uses indentations correctly.`
`TASK: [instruction]`
`CODE: [code]`

`Given an input task and a Python code, determine if the code uses quotes in string literals correctly.`
`TASK: [instruction]`
`CODE: [code]`

`Given an input task and a Python code, determine if the code uses duplicate parameters in a function.`
`TASK: [instruction]`
`CODE: [code]`

Table 2: Complete set of prompts. The tokens `[instruction]` and `[code]` are used to denote an instruction from the dataset and the corresponding generated code respectively.

SummEQuAL: Summarization Evaluation via Question Answering using Large Language Models

Junyuan Liu and **Zhengxiang Shi** and **Aldo Lipani**
University College London
{junyuan.liu.22,zhengxiang.shi.19,aldo.lipani}@ucl.ac.uk

Abstract

Summarization is hard to evaluate due to its diverse and abstract nature. Although N-gram-based metrics like BLEU and ROUGE are prevalent, they often do not align well with human evaluations. While model-based alternatives such as BERTScore improve, they typically require extensive labelled data. The advent of Large Language Models (LLMs) presents a promising avenue for evaluation. To this end, we introduce SummEQuAL, a novel content-based framework using LLMs for unified, reproducible summarization evaluation. SummEQuAL evaluates summaries by comparing their content with the source document, employing a question-answering approach to gauge both recall and precision. To validate SummEQuAL's effectiveness, we develop a dataset based on MultiWOZ. We conduct experiments on SummEval and our MultiWOZ-based dataset, showing that SummEQuAL largely improves the quality of summarization evaluation. Notably, SummEQuAL demonstrates a 19.7% improvement over QuestEval in terms of sample-level Pearson correlation with human assessments of consistency on the SummEval dataset. Furthermore, it exceeds the performance of the BERTScore baseline by achieving a 17.3% increase in Spearman correlation on our MultiWOZ-based dataset. Our study illuminates the potential of LLMs for a unified evaluation framework, setting a new paradigm for future summarization evaluation.

1 Introduction

Summary evaluation remains a complex task, and to this day, it cannot be adequately accomplished by automatic metrics (Chen et al., 2022; Goyal et al., 2022). While N-gram-based metrics like BLEU (Papineni et al., 2002) and ROUGE (Lin, 2004) are widely used, they often show a poor correlation with human judgment, particularly in content assessment (Kasai et al., 2022a; Reiter and Belz, 2009). In addition, these methods rely on references as a "gold standard", which diminishes their effectiveness especially when assessing varied and abstract summaries due to the limited availability of reference texts. Summary evaluation has higher requirements for diversity and accuracy.

The rise of Large Language Models (LLMs) offers a promising way to evaluate generative texts more effectively, due to their understanding and reasoning abilities. While previous studies have been conducted in various contexts, such as machine translation Kocmi and Federmann (2023) and summarization (Chen et al., 2023; Fu et al., 2023; Liu et al., 2023) (without relying on reference summaries), the use of LLMs for evaluation has its limitations. Specifically, there are large variation across different prompts and LLMs, which complicates the use of a unified evaluation framework. While the question-answering (QA) approach offers a structured method for evaluation to mitigate this issue, existing QA approaches still have several limitations (Durmus et al., 2020; Manakul et al., 2023; Scialom et al., 2021; Wang et al., 2020): (1) previous works are more confined to direct answers, and answers based on reasoning or hidden information are often tricky; (2) models in generating questions lack focus so they may introduce irrelevant information; and (3) models need expensive pre-training and the performance will be influenced by the coverage and quality of training data.

To address these issues, we propose a novel unified framework for summarization evaluation *SummEQuAL*, which can effectively identify abstract information across a wide range of topics and perform complex inference. Specifically, SummEQuAL streamlines the evaluation process by breaking it down into separate tasks and conducts QA to approximate human-like evaluation. It guides LLMs with a structured schema to identify key information and employs a QA mechanism to complete the content evaluation, producing more re-

Proceedings of the 2nd Workshop on Natural Language Reasoning and Structured Explanations (@ACL 2024), pages 46–55
August 15, 2024

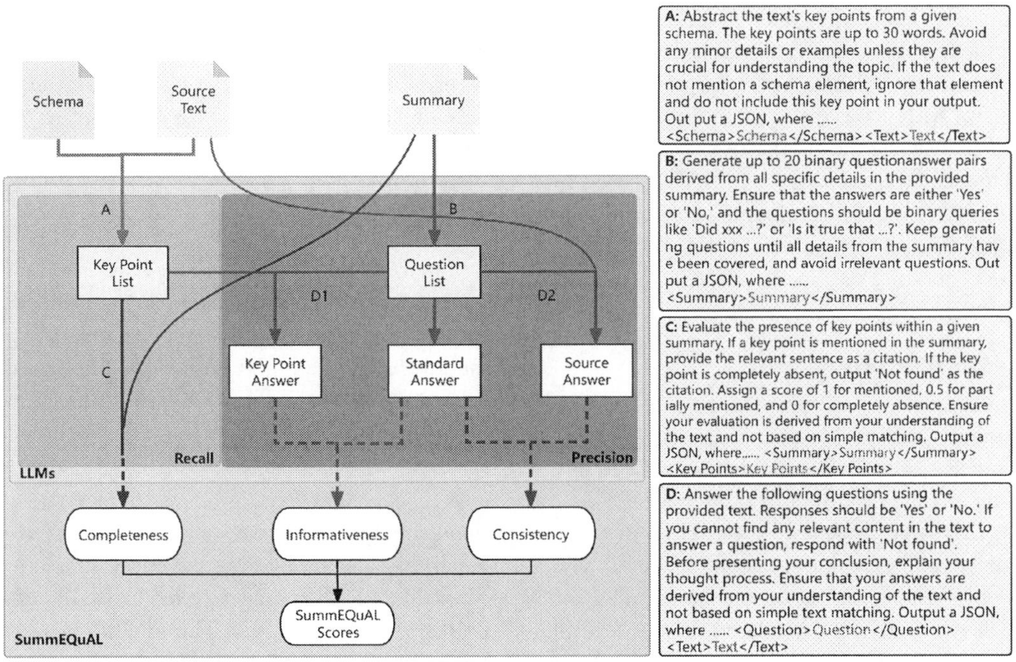

Figure 1: Illustration of the SummEQuAL framework. The blue and red areas represent the recall-oriented and the precision-oriented framework respectively. Solid colored lines and letters represent subtasks of LLMs. Other lines are simple comparison and calculation. The right side is an example of prompts for the subtasks.

liable results. Our experimental results on the SummEval dataset and MultiWOZ-based dataset demonstrate that the QA process benefits from LLMs. Particularly remarkable is that SummEQuAL improves the Spearman correlation with human evaluation by 19.7% on SummEval consistency, compared with our baseline QuestEval.

In summary, the main contributions of this paper are as follows:

1. We propose a unified summarization evaluation framework, SummEQuAL, for content correctness via QA using LLMs, minimising human works (§3).
2. We introduce a new dataset based on MultiWOZ to assess the quality of summarization content evaluation (§4.2).
3. As demonstrated in our experiments, our proposed framework, SummEQuAL, improves the baseline by 19.7% on the SummEval benchmark (§5.1.2) and 17.3% on the MultiWOZ-based dataset (§5.2.2).
4. Our further analysis reveals that LLMs can evaluate uniformly and robustly by designing a workflow with objective sub-tasks (§6).

2 Related Works

2.1 N-gram-based Evaluation Metrics

N-gram-based metrics measure the overlap between the generated summary and a reference summary. BLEU (Papineni et al., 2002) quantifies the concurrence of n-grams in a precision-oriented manner. ROUGE (Lin, 2004) assesses summarization from recall orientation. Since the above methods mainly focus on n-gram matching, they may fail to capture higher-level issues such as sentence structure, syntax, and semantics. Also, it can be affected by the repeated use of common phrases. As a result, they cannot accurately measure the content quality of a generated text (Reiter and Belz, 2009). Although many new metrics have appeared, nearly 70% of research works are still based on the old BLUE and ROUGE metrics (Kasai et al., 2022b).

2.2 Pre-trained Model-based Evaluation

Pre-trained model metrics are a category of methods that utilize pre-trained language models to evaluate. The language models can better capture semantic information and consequently assess the quality of generated text more accurately. BERTScore (Zhang et al., 2020) compares text embeddings, calculating similarity scores through the alignment of generated and reference summaries at a token level. MoverScore (Zhao et al., 2019) based on BERT considers the movement between words to evaluate the similarity between the generated text and the reference text. BARTScore (Yuan et al., 2021) regards evaluation as a text generation problem, which calculates the probability of a text generating or generated from other texts to evaluate.

2.3 QA-based Evaluation

A direct approach to compare the information of summaries and source documents is through the QA process. Previous research has explored this in fine-tuned language models. SummaQA (Scialom et al., 2019) generates questions from the source document and compares the confidence of the QA model in answering based on the summary, but fake answers are not considered. FEQA (Durmus et al., 2020) and QAGS (Wang et al., 2020), from another angle, generate questions from summarizations, using the original text for answering, to evaluate factual consistency. QuestEval (Scialom et al., 2021) subsequently applied QA in both directions, and MQAG (Manakul et al., 2023) introduced a multiple-choice QA model to deal with highly abstractive summarizations or multiple-answer spans.

2.4 LLM-based Evaluation

LLMs have been pre-trained on vast text data, enabling them to address a variety of domains without specific training. They can identify complex logical content. GPTscore (Fu et al., 2023) utilizes LLMs for zero-shot instruction and in-context learning, suggesting that higher-quality texts are generated with a higher likelihood. Incorporating CoT (Wei et al., 2022), G-EVAL (Liu et al., 2023) yields superior outcomes, allowing LLMs to autonomously generate evaluation methods. There's a bias observed favouring LLM-created content. Additionally, Chen et al. (Chen et al., 2023) determined that explicit LLM evaluations are more effective than implicit ones. In conclusion, while LLMs offer promising capabilities in text evaluation, challenges such as sensitivity, model bias, and score distribution bias remain.

3 SummEQuAL Framework

We propose a QA-based framework utilizing LLMs to evaluate summarization systems without needing human references for each summary. SummEQuAL incorporates both recall-oriented and precision-oriented approaches, featuring three submetrics, as illustrated in Figure 1. Below, we provide detailed explanations for each metric in our framework.

3.1 Completeness

Summarization aims to extract core information from texts to present the main content of the original text in a shorter form. A good summary should include as much important information from the original text as possible. Based on this concept, we first consider how much important information from the original text is included in the summary.

A *schema* module is introduced to facilitate question generation from the source texts. Rather than generating questions from the entire source texts, we utilize LLMs to generate a concise list of key points with the schema. The schema is a set of predefined important information for certain summarization tasks, which includes important information such as the main character of a story, the purpose of a product, or the time required to reserve a restaurant table, depending on the purpose and topic of the summarization. Experts can define schema according to their professional knowledge about the purpose of a summarization task. In this way, we do not need to create references for all summaries but only design one schema for one summarization task. Also, it is possible to generate the schema by LLMs with the description of the task topic. An example of schema for news is:

```
{
  "Time": "When does the event happen?",
  "Location": "Where does the event happen?",
  "Figure": "Who are the participants involved?",
  "Description": "What is the main event?",
  "Cause": "Why does the main event happen?",
  "Result": "What are the results of the event?"
}
```

LLMs generate the list of key points by the schema, and then compare whether these key points are included in the summary. The comparison is presented by a match function M, of which the value is between 0 and 1. A simple way is to answer boolean questions by LLMs like "Is it included in the summary that ...", and then transform it into numbers. Given a key point list K including n key points k_1 ... k_n, and a summary S, we define the *completeness* (Cons.) of a summary as:

$$\texttt{Comp.} = \frac{1}{n}\sum_{i=1}^{n} M(S, k_i), \quad (1)$$

3.2 Informativeness

A good summary should also avoid incorporating irrelevant information, and ideally, all the information within summaries should be of significance. In evaluation, we employ LLMs to generate question-answer pairs pertaining to the details of summaries. Subsequently, we prompt LLMs to answer questions using a key point list and then assess whether the answers to the two sets of questions match. To streamline the comparison process, we also generate boolean questions in the experiments of this paper. Denote the question list generated from summary S by LLMs as $Q(S)$, and q are questions in it. Given a text T and a question q, the answer generated by LLMs is $A(T, q)$. We define *informativeness* (Inf.) as:

$$\texttt{Inf.} = \frac{1}{|Q(S)|} \sum_{q \in Q(S)} \delta(A(S,q), A(K,q)), \quad (2)$$

where $|\cdot|$ represents the size of the set and $\delta(a, b)$ is equal to 1 when $a = b$ otherwise 0.

3.3 Consistency

Generative models could mistakenly create information that seems plausible but is not right, known as hallucinations. In the summarization task, this property introduces information outside the source document, thus damaging the consistency of the summary with the source document. To measure consistency, we use the summary to generate question-answer pairs, then answer the question by the source text with LLMs. After these, we compare the two sets of answers. For a given source document D, *consistency* (Cons.) is defined as:

$$\texttt{Cons.} = \frac{1}{|Q(S)|} \sum_{q \in Q(S)} \delta(A(S,q), A(D,q)) \quad (3)$$

3.4 SummEQuAL Score

SummEQuAL score is a comprehensive index combining completeness, informativeness, and consistency. The equation is structured to reflect the correct proportion of important and effective information. Completeness and informativeness are combined using the harmonic mean to balance the quantity and relevance of information. Consistency is then used as a multiplier to calculate the correction rate, reflecting the amount of accurate information in the summary. SummEQuAL score is computed as follows:

$$\texttt{SummEQuAL} = 2 \cdot \frac{\texttt{Comp} \cdot \texttt{Inf}}{\texttt{Comp} + \texttt{Inf}} \cdot \texttt{Cons} \quad (4)$$

4 Datasets

4.1 SummEval

SummEval (Fabbri et al., 2021) is one of the largest human annotated datasets for summarization evaluation tasks, built on the foundation of the CNN/-Daily Mail (Hermann et al., 2015) dataset. SummEval collects and releases both expert and crowd-sourced human evaluation for 16 model outputs on 100 articles across 4 dimensions to advance research into human-correlated evaluation metrics. For each summary, there are 3 expert and 5 crowd-sourced evaluations, totalling 12,800 human annotations. We will compare the correlation between LLMs' evaluations within the SummEQuAL framework and human evaluations in this dataset.

4.2 MultiWOZ

MultiWOZ (Budzianowski et al., 2018) is an open dataset released by the University of Cambridge, serving as a widely-used multi-domain task-oriented dialogue dataset with detailed human annotations for tracking dialogue information. As a task-oriented dataset, MultiWOZ offers objective schemas for specific tasks and annotated slot values for all dialogues. The dataset presents complex logic and multiple topics within individual dialogue texts, making it suitable for evaluating the framework's proficiency in working with a designed schema. We choose the newest version MultiWOZ 2.4 (Ye et al., 2022) for the experiment.

Dataset Construction Task-oriented summarization focuses on specific results. For booking tickets, we expect the summaries to fully contain information on user demands and the booking result. With this in mind, we created summaries on the MultiWOZ dataset and manually evaluated the completeness of the summaries. We randomly sample 50 dialogues from the test set of the MultiWOZ 2.4 dataset, and generate both short summaries and detailed summaries for each dialogue using the text-curie-001 model, GPT-3.5-turbo-0613 model, and GPT-4 model (OpenAI, 2023), totalling 300 summaries. The statistics of the dialogues and the summaries are shown in Table 1. Then, we annotated the summaries' completeness by checking how much proportion of the schema information was contained to provide a score. We used three annotators for marking. If the annotations by the first

Table 1: Statistics for dialogue and summary. The lengths are described by the number of words.

Dialogue		Average Summary Lengths	
Metric	Value	Summarization	Length
Dialogue Turn	6.98	gpt-3.5 simple	109.7
Mean Length	205.8	gpt-3.5 detailed	126.5
Min. Length	70	gpt-4 simple	69.0
Max. Length	470	gpt-4 detailed	89.9
Median Length	210	text-curie-001 simple	68.7
Std. Deviation	81.2	text-curie-001 detailed	72.7

two annotators were inconsistent, the third annotator adjudicated to determine the final annotation.

5 Experiments and Results

Evaluation Strategy. We evaluate automatic metrics by comparing their alignment with reference human evaluations. Three prevalent correlations, the Spearman correlation, the Person correlation and the Kendall's Tau correlation are employed. Given n source texts and m summary models, the i-th text's summary generated by the j-th model is denoted as $s_{i,j}$. The formula of correlation at a sample level is as follows:

$$\text{Corr} = \frac{1}{n}\sum_{i=1}^{n}\rho\left([e_{\text{auto}}(s_{i,1}), \ldots, e_{\text{auto}}(s_{i,M})], [e_{\text{ref}}(s_{i,1}), \ldots, e_{\text{ref}}(s_{i,M})]\right) \quad (5)$$

where ρ denotes the function of correlation metrics. e_{auto} and e_{ref} denote the automatic evaluation and reference evaluation functions, respectively.

5.1 Evaluation on SummEval

5.1.1 Experimental Setup

We evaluate the summaries in SummEval dataset with our SummEQuAL framework and compare the evaluation results with human evaluations. In this paper, if not specified, we use the GPT-3.5-turbo-0613 model with a temperature of 0 as the LLM of our framework, since other LLMs do not always follow the instructions strictly to work with the SummEQuAL framework. To avoid confusion across texts, each step of our framework separately inputs data into the LLM and is linked by processing output JSON. The human evaluation is set using the average scores from three experts. The determined input schema is the same as the example schema shown in Section 3.1. To make the evaluation for our framework convincing, we also use a rephrased version of the prompts besides the example prompts in Figure 1 and calculate the average correlation.

5.1.2 Results

LLMs have demonstrated competitive results within the SummEQuAL framework in Table 2. On the aspect of consistency, SummEQuAL has shown a clear superiority over traditional automatic metrics, improving by 19.7% compared with the best-performing QA models and more than 10% compared with G-EVAL. SummEQuAl benefits both from LLMs and QA process, effectively verifying whether the information in the summary is consistent with the original text.

In terms of relevance, the correlations are high on G-EVAL and QuestEval. The primary reason for not outstanding results lies in the differences in the definitions of relevance. SummEQuAL scores does not precisely reflect the definition of relevance in SummEval, which emphasizes selecting important content from the source without stressing correctness. In contrast, G-EVAL directly prompt the definition of relevance. QuestEval, when utilizing summaries to answer questions generated from the original text, relies on the answerability confidence instead of an answer, thus aligning more closely with the definition of relevance in SummEval.

5.2 Task-oriented Summarization Evaluation

Task-oriented summarization requires a focus on specific information within the text. For instance, in ticket booking dialogues, details about the ticket such as time and location are crucial, while in a doctor's diagnostic interview notes, the patient's symptoms and feelings are of importance. To accurately evaluate the effectiveness of task-oriented summarization, a well-defined schema that lists all the relevant information is helpful. SummEQuAL can then be used to provide a desirable evaluation for the tasks, ensuring that the summarization meets the specific requirements. To test the ability of the SummEQuAL framework on task-oriented summarization evaluation, we build a MultiWOZ-based dataset, which contains dialogues between users and conversational systems, involving a range of tasks, such as restaurant reservations, travel bookings, information queries, and so forth, and then we conduct experiments with the SummEQuAL framework.

5.2.1 Experimental Setup

A dictionary with the 35 types of slots tracked in the dialogue dataset is set as the schema for generating key points. Within the SummEQuAL framework, we input schemas into both the GPT-3.5 and

Table 2: Sample-level Spearman correlation (Spear.), Pearson correlation (Pear.), and Kendall's Tau correlation (Kend.) of relevance and consistency on SummEval. #Ref. is the number of reference summaries in evaluation. Results of QA metrics are from Scialom's work (Scialom et al., 2021).

Metrics	#Ref.	Relevance			Consistency		
		Spear.	Pear.	Kend.	Spear.	Pear.	Kend.
ROUGE-1	1	0.199	0.220	0.152	0.157	0.200	0.132
ROUGE-2	1	0.145	0.174	0.105	0.137	0.162	0.116
ROUGE-L	1	0.203	0.221	0.156	0.149	0.198	0.125
ROUGE-1	11	0.311	0.347	0.237	0.153	0.216	0.125
ROUGE-2	11	0.248	0.298	0.189	0.122	0.181	0.101
ROUGE-L	11	0.293	0.329	0.224	0.103	0.180	0.082
BERTScore	11	0.269	0.304	0.203	0.168	0.242	0.140
BARTScore	11	0.264	0.290	0.197	0.311	0.321	0.256
MoverScore	11	0.282	0.313	0.215	0.166	0.221	0.137
SummaQA	0	–	0.262	–	–	0.083	–
QAGS	0	–	0.204	–	–	0.091	–
QuestEval	0	–	**0.392**	–	–	0.420	–
G-EVAL-3.5	0	**0.385**	–	**0.293**	0.386	–	0.318
SummEQuAL	0	0.311	0.337	0.241	0.274	0.324	0.227
-Completeness	0	0.252	0.274	0.204	0.151	0.182	0.131
-Informativeness	0	0.181	0.187	0.143	0.161	0.188	0.136
-Consistency	0	0.228	0.265	0.193	**0.432**	**0.503**	**0.403**

GPT-4 models, generating two lists of key points. To evaluate the LLMs' capability to generate key points based on the schema, we manually compared these generated lists against the slot values annotated in MultiWOZ. Considering the target of this ticket-booking summarization, only slot values in the final turn of user-system dialogues are extracted as the ground truth. After this, we use a simple match, ROUGE-L, BERTscore and LLMs to compare the key point list with the source document (C in Figure 1) and generate a completeness score. We compared these completeness scores with human scores to demonstrate whether this framework benefits from LLMs. Last but not least, we compare the performance of different evaluation metrics like ROUGE, BERTScore and BARTScore on the 300 summaries consisting of simple and detailed summaries generated by the text-curie-001, the GPT-3.5-turbo-0613 and GPT-4 models. Based on our observation, the GPT-4 model is better than the GPT-3.5 model, and both outperform the text-curie-001 model; the detailed version is better than the simple version of the same model. So we assigned them scores from high to low as ground truth. Finally, we calculated the correlation coefficients of metrics and assigned scores accordingly.

5.2.2 Results

As shown in Table 3, both models can extract key points according to the schema with relatively good results, highlighting the flexibility and adaptability of the SummEQuAL framework. If the schema is given, GPT-3.5 with relatively weak reasoning ability can obtain high recall. Compared with GPT-4, the precision of GPT-3.5 is lower. We checked the output and found this is because some unimportant information outside the schema is introduced, which is often repeated information or redundant content as a result of not correctly following the schema.

Table 4 shows that the evaluation of the SummEQuAL framework benefits from the reasoning ability of LLMs. The comparison based on LLMs is the most consistent with human evaluations, surpassing

Table 3: Key Point Generation Abilities: Scores are derived by comparing model predictions with the last dialogue turn's state value manually.

Model	Recall	Precision	F1
GPT-3.5	0.919	0.758	0.830
GPT-4	0.958	0.875	0.915

Table 4: Key Point Comparison Abilities: Model correlation with human on comparison of key point and summary.

Model	Spearman	Pearson	Kendall Tau
Simple match	0.298	0.229	0.211
ROUGE-L	0.328	0.282	0.232
BERTScore	0.644	0.634	0.476
GPT-3.5	0.742	0.756	0.599
GPT-4	**0.929**	**0.828**	**0.946**

Table 5: Sample-level Correlations of Summarization Evaluation on Our MultiWOZ-based Dataset.

Metrics	Spear.	Pear.	Kend.
ROUGE-1	-0.010	0.077	-0.007
ROUGE-L	0.003	0.079	0.001
BERTScore	0.589	0.657	0.489
BARTScore	0.423	0.519	0.317
MoverScore	-0.137	-0.360	-0.109
QuestEval	0.511	0.568	0.429
SummEQuAL	0.240	0.283	0.192
-Completeness	**0.691**	**0.764**	**0.573**
-Informativeness	0.212	0.257	0.161
-Consistency	-0.028	-0.058	-0.031

other methods significantly. Upon careful observation of the results, we discovered that GPT-3.5 tends to make errors and give lower scores, which suggests that in complex scenarios, GPT-3.5's reasoning ability may not be sufficient to capture all the details of the summaries. We will discuss this in the analysis section (§6) in detail.

By the comparison in Table 5, the completeness of SummEQuAL has achieved the best correlation, but the correlations of other parts are not high. Metrics based on pre-trained language models perform well, but ROUGE performs poorly. This result is from the generation of summarization. The GPT models tend to cover more content when summarizing on MultiWOZ, so the summarization contains comprehensive important information but is not concise. Moreover, since both GPT-3.5 and GPT-4 have good summary capabilities for the MultiWOZ data set, the actual summarization quality of GPT-3.5 is not lower than GPT-4 in some cases, especially considering the consistency. As a result, the assigned scores are not completely accurate, which affects the overall correlation coefficient.

6 Further Analysis

6.1 Discrepancy of Summarization Tasks

The evaluation result is affected by the dataset's features, the evaluation criteria and the evaluation target. Articles in SummEval are longer and contain more detailed descriptions, making it easier for summarizations to introduce non-essential information and produce inconsistent information, while the dialogues are shorter. Moreover, we need to consider the practical meaning of the comparison scores. The dialogues in MultiWOZ are based on specific tasks, and their themes and key information are more clearly defined. In the case of providing a schema reflecting the content of the task as a reference, the completeness score is more consistent with the target of evaluation. When using SummEQuAL for evaluation tasks, we can clarify the purpose of the task and use a more appropriate schema and metric or combination of metrics for a better evaluation.

6.2 Error Analysis

Inferencing capability. As illustrated in Table 6, the dialogue contains implicit shifts of needed information. GPT-3.5 only capture the user's initial request for a restaurant serving canapes and did not correctly comprehend the system's rejection of the user's proposed dining time of 16:15. This comparison underscores the importance of inferencing abilities of the model's reasoning capabilities. Similar errors could also occur in the evaluation of informativeness and consistency.

Subjectivity. Evaluation on the SummEval dataset is influenced significantly by subjectivity. The evaluation results can vary depending on the chosen schema. Our schema may focus on different information from the human annotation in SummEval. Consequently, the generated key points do not align with information in the reference summaries used by human experts during evaluation, resulting in a potential distortion of the summarization evaluation.

Stability. When generating key points, GPT-3.5 could generate duplicate information or possible schema values that do not appear in the summary, causing the SummEQuAL framework to fail. During the entire evaluation process, GPT-3.5 is occasionally affected by the text content, so that it is unable to correctly execute the framework tasks according to the instructions, and outputs wrong or incomplete content.

6.3 Reproducibility

An inherent characteristic of LLMs, especially when interfaced through APIs, is the potential variability in their outputs upon repeated experiments. We evaluate the potential difference level of this issue by repeating the experiment. Here we use the GPT-3.5-turbo as the base model of the SummEQuAL framework, and we experimented on the SummEval benchmark. Table 7 shows that the majority of the results across various metrics fell within the minimal absolute difference percentage

Table 6: Case Study: Comparison of GPT-3.5 and GPT-4 for Key Points Generation. Table (top) provides a brief overview of the dialogue and Table (bottom) summarizes both the actual key points and the predictions. Key points highlighted in green indicate correct summarization, while those in red represent incorrect predictions by the model.

Role	Dialogue
User:	I am looking for a restaurant that serves canapes in the east.
Sys:	Unfortunately there are no restaurants serving canapes in the east.
User:	Ah, well, too bad. In that case, I think that'll be everything that I needed. Thanks and have a good day!
Sys:	Are you sure? I can find other options in other parts of town?
User:	How about Italian food?
Sys:	There is the Pizza Hut Fen Ditton in the east serving Italian food.
User:	Great! Please book a table for 6 at 16:15 on Saturday.
Sys:	Sorry, but no tables are available for that time slot. Would you like to change the time?
User:	How about 15:15 then?
Sys:	Your table is booked. Your reference number is qw8jzwzk. Can I help you with anything else?
User:	Great. Thank you for your help today. That is all.

Key Points (Name)	Slot Values (Truth)	GPT-3.5 (Prediction)	GPT-4 (Prediction)
restaurant-food	italian	canapes	italian
restaurant-area	east	east	east
restaurant-book day	saturday	saturday	saturday
restaurant-book people	6	6	6
restaurant-book time	15:15	16:15	15:15
restaurant-name	pizza hut fenditton	pizza hut fen ditton	pizza hut fen ditton

Table 7: Comparison of Repeated Experiment Results

Metrics	Abs Mean	Variance	Abs Difference Percentage				
			0-0.1	0.1-0.2	0.2-0.3	0.3-0.4	>0.4
S.E.	0.050	0.010	81.31%	11.75%	4.31%	1.69%	0.94%
Comp.	0.052	0.012	78.94%	11.69%	5.69%	2.38%	1.31%
Inf.	0.056	0.016	78.75%	10.19%	5.62%	3.81%	1.62%
Cons.	0.018	0.004	92.31%	4.56%	2.06%	0.75%	0.31%

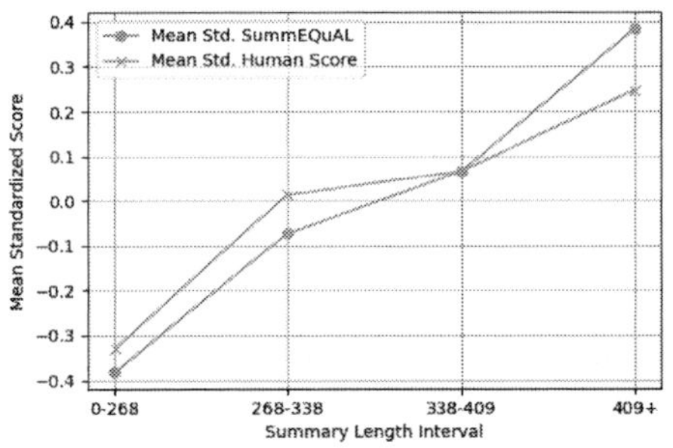

Figure 2: Standardized SummEQuAL and Human Scores by Summary Length Interval

range (0-0.1), indicating a high degree of reproducibility. Among all the metrics, the consistency score shows the smallest discrepancy.

6.4 Comparison of Text Length

We conduct a comparative analysis with human scores to evaluate the possible bias of our SummEQuAL score across various text lengths. First, we scale the SummEQuAL and human scores using z-score normalization to ensure comparability. We then grouped the summaries into four equal-sized intervals based on length and computed the mean standardized score for both SummEQuAL and human evaluations within each group. Figure 2 indicates a general trend where both SummEQuAL and human scores increased with the length of the text. The apparent preference in the SummEQuAL model for longer texts could result from the fact that longer summaries are better in the SummEval benchmark. The overall parallel trends in SummEQuAL and human scoring across different text lengths demonstrate a degree of consistency.

7 Conclusion

This work proposes a novel summarization evaluation framework, SummEQuAL, based on LLMs. The SummEQuAL framework provides a reliable and effective approach for the evaluation of summarization, opening up a new direction for future work on unified and reproducible summarization evaluation using LLMs. SummEQuAL sheds new light on developing reliable and consistent summarization evaluation methods, expected to help researchers more precisely understand and evaluate the performance of summarization models, thereby improving the quality of summarization content.

Limitations

SummEQuAL's performance depends on the capabilities of LLMs. Any limitations these LLMs have, especially in parsing complex logic or discerning implicit information, will directly influence SummEQuAL's evaluation. The framework's reliance on multi-step reasoning, involving several interactions, means it can be time-intensive and resource-heavy compared to simpler one-step evaluations. Moreover, although SummEQuAL has shown promise in initial tests, its effectiveness across different models, languages, and text domains still needs further evaluation.

References

Paweł Budzianowski, Tsung-Hsien Wen, Bo-Hsiang Tseng, Iñigo Casanueva, Stefan Ultes, Osman Ramadan, and Milica Gašić. 2018. MultiWOZ - a large-scale multi-domain Wizard-of-Oz dataset for task-oriented dialogue modelling. In *Proceedings of the 2018 Conference on Empirical Methods in Natural Language Processing*, pages 5016–5026, Brussels, Belgium. Association for Computational Linguistics.

Yi Chen, Rui Wang, Haiyun Jiang, Shuming Shi, and Ruifeng Xu. 2023. Exploring the use of large language models for reference-free text quality evaluation: A preliminary empirical study. *ArXiv preprint*, abs/2304.00723.

Yulong Chen, Naihao Deng, Yang Liu, and Yue Zhang. 2022. DialogSum challenge: Results of the dialogue summarization shared task. In *Proceedings of the 15th International Conference on Natural Language Generation: Generation Challenges*, pages 94–103, Waterville, Maine, USA and virtual meeting. Association for Computational Linguistics.

Esin Durmus, He He, and Mona Diab. 2020. FEQA: A question answering evaluation framework for faithfulness assessment in abstractive summarization. In *Proceedings of the 58th Annual Meeting of the Association for Computational Linguistics*, pages 5055–5070, Online. Association for Computational Linguistics.

Alexander R. Fabbri, Wojciech Kryściński, Bryan McCann, Caiming Xiong, Richard Socher, and Dragomir Radev. 2021. SummEval: Re-evaluating summarization evaluation. *Transactions of the Association for Computational Linguistics*, 9:391–409.

Jinlan Fu, See-Kiong Ng, Zhengbao Jiang, and Pengfei Liu. 2023. Gptscore: Evaluate as you desire. *ArXiv preprint*, abs/2302.04166.

Tanya Goyal, Junyi Jessy Li, and Greg Durrett. 2022. News summarization and evaluation in the era of gpt-3. *ArXiv preprint*, abs/2209.12356.

Karl Moritz Hermann, Tomás Kociský, Edward Grefenstette, Lasse Espeholt, Will Kay, Mustafa Suleyman, and Phil Blunsom. 2015. Teaching machines to read and comprehend. In *Advances in Neural Information Processing Systems 28: Annual Conference on Neural Information Processing Systems 2015, December 7-12, 2015, Montreal, Quebec, Canada*, pages 1693–1701.

Jungo Kasai, Keisuke Sakaguchi, Ronan Le Bras, Lavinia Dunagan, Jacob Morrison, Alexander Fabbri, Yejin Choi, and Noah A. Smith. 2022a. Bidimensional leaderboards: Generate and evaluate language hand in hand. In *Proceedings of the 2022 Conference of the North American Chapter of the Association for Computational Linguistics: Human Language Technologies*, pages 3540–3557, Seattle, United States. Association for Computational Linguistics.

Jungo Kasai, Keisuke Sakaguchi, Ronan Le Bras, Lavinia Dunagan, Jacob Morrison, Alexander Fabbri, Yejin Choi, and Noah A. Smith. 2022b. Bidimensional leaderboards: Generate and evaluate language hand in hand. In *Proceedings of the 2022 Conference of the North American Chapter of the Association for Computational Linguistics: Human Language Technologies*, pages 3540–3557, Seattle, United States. Association for Computational Linguistics.

Tom Kocmi and Christian Federmann. 2023. Large language models are state-of-the-art evaluators of translation quality. *ArXiv preprint*, abs/2302.14520.

Chin-Yew Lin. 2004. ROUGE: A package for automatic evaluation of summaries. In *Text Summarization Branches Out*, pages 74–81, Barcelona, Spain. Association for Computational Linguistics.

Yang Liu, Dan Iter, Yichong Xu, Shuohang Wang, Ruochen Xu, and Chenguang Zhu. 2023. G-eval: NLG evaluation using gpt-4 with better human alignment. In *Proceedings of the 2023 Conference on Empirical Methods in Natural Language Processing*, pages 2511–2522, Singapore. Association for Computational Linguistics.

Potsawee Manakul, Adian Liusie, and Mark JF Gales. 2023. Mqag: Multiple-choice question answering and generation for assessing information consistency in summarization. *ArXiv preprint*, abs/2301.12307.

OpenAI. 2023. Openai platform models documentation. Accessed: 2023-10-02.

Kishore Papineni, Salim Roukos, Todd Ward, and Wei-Jing Zhu. 2002. Bleu: a method for automatic evaluation of machine translation. In *Proceedings of the 40th Annual Meeting of the Association for Computational Linguistics*, pages 311–318, Philadelphia, Pennsylvania, USA. Association for Computational Linguistics.

Ehud Reiter and Anja Belz. 2009. An investigation into the validity of some metrics for automatically evaluating natural language generation systems. *Computational Linguistics*, 35(4):529–558.

Thomas Scialom, Paul-Alexis Dray, Sylvain Lamprier, Benjamin Piwowarski, Jacopo Staiano, Alex Wang, and Patrick Gallinari. 2021. QuestEval: Summarization asks for fact-based evaluation. In *Proceedings of the 2021 Conference on Empirical Methods in Natural Language Processing*, pages 6594–6604, Online and Punta Cana, Dominican Republic. Association for Computational Linguistics.

Thomas Scialom, Sylvain Lamprier, Benjamin Piwowarski, and Jacopo Staiano. 2019. Answers unite! unsupervised metrics for reinforced summarization models. In *Proceedings of the 2019 Conference on Empirical Methods in Natural Language Processing and the 9th International Joint Conference on Natural Language Processing (EMNLP-IJCNLP)*, pages 3246–3256, Hong Kong, China. Association for Computational Linguistics.

Alex Wang, Kyunghyun Cho, and Mike Lewis. 2020. Asking and answering questions to evaluate the factual consistency of summaries. In *Proceedings of the 58th Annual Meeting of the Association for Computational Linguistics*, pages 5008–5020, Online. Association for Computational Linguistics.

Jason Wei, Xuezhi Wang, Dale Schuurmans, Maarten Bosma, Fei Xia, Ed H Chi, Quoc V Le, Denny Zhou, et al. 2022. Chain-of-thought prompting elicits reasoning in large language models. In *Advances in Neural Information Processing Systems*.

Fanghua Ye, Jarana Manotumruksa, and Emine Yilmaz. 2022. MultiWOZ 2.4: A multi-domain task-oriented dialogue dataset with essential annotation corrections to improve state tracking evaluation. In *Proceedings of the 23rd Annual Meeting of the Special Interest Group on Discourse and Dialogue*, pages 351–360, Edinburgh, UK. Association for Computational Linguistics.

Weizhe Yuan, Graham Neubig, and Pengfei Liu. 2021. Bartscore: Evaluating generated text as text generation. In *Advances in Neural Information Processing Systems 34: Annual Conference on Neural Information Processing Systems 2021, NeurIPS 2021, December 6-14, 2021, virtual*, pages 27263–27277.

Tianyi Zhang, Varsha Kishore, Felix Wu, Kilian Q. Weinberger, and Yoav Artzi. 2020. Bertscore: Evaluating text generation with BERT. In *8th International Conference on Learning Representations, ICLR 2020, Addis Ababa, Ethiopia, April 26-30, 2020*. OpenReview.net.

Wei Zhao, Maxime Peyrard, Fei Liu, Yang Gao, Christian M. Meyer, and Steffen Eger. 2019. MoverScore: Text generation evaluating with contextualized embeddings and earth mover distance. In *Proceedings of the 2019 Conference on Empirical Methods in Natural Language Processing and the 9th International Joint Conference on Natural Language Processing (EMNLP-IJCNLP)*, pages 563–578, Hong Kong, China. Association for Computational Linguistics.

LOGIC-LM++: Multi-Step Refinement for Symbolic Formulations

Shashank Kirtania, Priyanshu Gupta, Arjun Radhakrishna
Microsoft
{t-skirtania, priyansgupta, arradha} @microsoft.com

Abstract

In this paper we examine the limitations of Large Language Models (LLMs) for complex reasoning tasks. Although recent works have started to employ formal languages as an intermediate representation for reasoning tasks, they often face challenges in accurately generating and refining these formal specifications to ensure correctness. To address these issues, this paper proposes Logic-LM++, an improvement on Logic-LM (Pan et al., 2023). It uses the ability of LLMs to do pairwise comparisons, allowing the evaluation of the refinements suggested by the LLM. The paper demonstrates that Logic-LM++ outperforms Logic-LM and other contemporary techniques across natural language reasoning tasks on three datasets, FOLIO, ProofWriter and AR-LSAT, with an average improvement of 18.5% on standard prompting, 12.3% on chain of thought prompting and 5% on Logic-LM.

1 Introduction

Large language models (LLMs) have shown proven capability of reasoning (Brown et al., 2020; Chowdhery et al., 2022) but still struggle at complex reasoning problems as seen in real world assessments (Zhong et al., 2021). For complex multi hop reasoning tasks current state of the art approaches (Pan et al., 2023; Ye et al., 2023) leverage formal languages as intermediate representation of these reasoning problems and utilize symbolic reasoners to come up with the right response. A typical workflow of such techniques consist of 3 steps: a natural language prompt which consist of the task information, a response formulation for the problem, final response generated with symbolic executor.

While logic-assisted LLM reasoning techniques are promising, we observe following problems in such systems: Firstly, LLMs are poor at generating intermediate formal specifications. A few techniques try to counter this problem with a refinement loop (Madaan et al., 2023a; Welleck et al., 2022; Shinn et al., 2023) to improve upon the syntactical correctness of the symbolic formulation. Secondly, the LLMs are poor at repairing the formal representations with limited information with error information. For example, in Figure 1 the LLM initially generates a syntactically incorrect formulation. After a turn of refinement, while the LLM is able to generate a response that is syntactically correct, it introduces a *semantic* error in the formulation by incorrectly translating the statement "No young person teaches". These kind of incorrect translations from Natural Language (NL) to intermediate formal specifications is a common problem we observe over the failing cases of refinement. Thirdly, we observe that refinements are not always linear-resolving an error with the symbolic formulation can take multiple steps of careful edits and evaluation. The formulations generated in refinement stage in 1 introduced the wrong interpretation of "No young person teaches" to "All young people teaches".
To address these challenges we propose to add following measures in Logic-LM to enhance it's capabilities resulting in improved variant Logic-LM++.

We leverage the ability of LLMs to do pairwise comparison (Zheng et al., 2023a), this gives us an opportunity to evaluate the refinements suggested by the LLM and do a semantic check with respect to the problem statement to ensure if the edits in the symbolic formulation generated while refinement improve the formulation semantically not just syntactically.

We also improve on the refinement mechanism present in Logic-LM to give more context of the problem statement during refinement stage, this eliminates cases where recommended edits are appalling and do not improve the formulation significantly.

Proceedings of the 2nd Workshop on Natural Language Reasoning and Structured Explanations (@ACL 2024), pages 56–63

2 Related Work

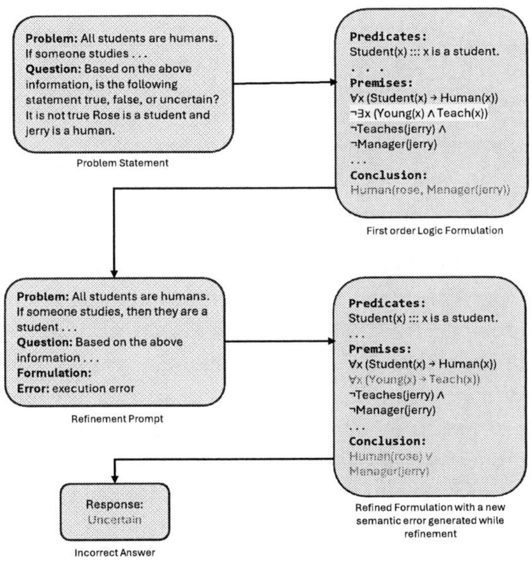

Figure 1: Refinement of logical formulations in Logic-LM

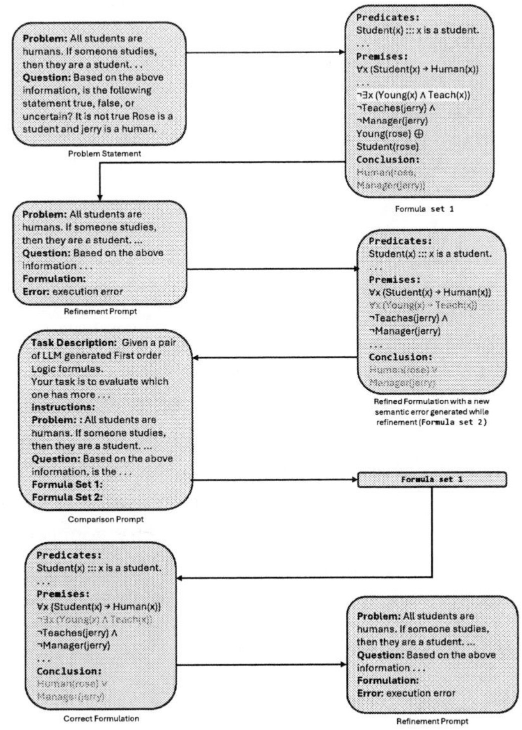

Figure 2: Improvement in refinement by Logic-LM++

2.1 Reasoning with LLMs

Large Language model (LLM) - based reasoning techniques commonly entail the deconstruction of complex questions into a sequence of intermediate steps, often referred to as chains, before reaching the ultimate solution. This technique is a reflection of methods such as Chain of Thought (CoT) prompting and its variations, as shown in various studies (Wei et al., 2022; Kojima et al., 2022). These methodologies require the meticulous segmentation of a problem into a chain of smaller, manageable chunks. Each of these chunks represents a step in the reasoning process, guiding the model towards a comprehensive solution. The concept of the reflection loop, as explored in previous research (Shinn et al., 2023; Madaan et al., 2023b), offers a means of refining the reasoning by identifying and eliminating any flaws that may be introduced by the LLM during a reasoning step. This process enhances the inherent capability of the LLM to self-correct, contributing to more accurate and reliable outcomes. Recent works have further explore the process of self-evaluation at these intermediate steps (Welleck et al., 2022; Paul et al., 2024). This process involves the LLM assessing its reasoning at each step, allowing it to identify any inaccuracies. By rectifying these issues before proceeding to the next step, the LLM can ensure a more accurate and reliable chain of reasoning. Aligned with our objective of capturing the natural language intent of the user from symbolic formulations, recent works (Endres et al., 2024) have also explored the translation of natural language into formal language post conditions. This research investigates how effectively we can convert the often-ambiguous language of human conversation into the precise, unambiguous language of formal logic. This translation process is crucial for the accurate interpretation and execution of user intent, particularly in complex or technical tasks.

2.2 Tool-augmented Large Language Models

Language models face inherent limitations, unable to access real-time data, execute actions, or conduct precise mathematical reasoning.To address this, recent research endeavors have sought to augment language models by integrating external resources such as retrievers (Nakano et al., 2021; Shi et al., 2023; Lazaridou et al., 2022), calculators (Cobbe et al., 2021), code interpreters (Wang et al., 2022), planners (Liu et al., 2023), symbolic solvers (Ye et al., 2023; Pan et al., 2023), and other pretrained models (Shen et al., 2023). Notably, in the realm of mathematical reasoning, numerous investigations

Dataset	GPT-3.5 Turbo				GPT-4			
	Standard	**CoT**	**Logic-LM**	**Logic-LM++**	**Standard**	**CoT**	**Logic-LM**	**Logic-LM++**
FOLIO	45.09	57.35	**62.80**	*62.25*	69.11	70.58	78.92	**84.80**
ProofWriter	35.50	49.17	58.33	**58.83**	52.67	68.11	79.66	79.66
AR-LSAT	20.34	17.31	26.41	**28.13**	33.33	35.06	43.04	**46.32**

Table 1: Accuracy of standard promoting, chain-of-thought (CoT) promoting, Logic-LM and Logic-LM++.

have illustrated the efficacy of incorporating calculators (Cobbe et al., 2021; Imani et al., 2023) or Python interpreters (Gao et al., 2023; Chen et al., 2022) into language models, significantly enhancing performance by offloading numerical computations. Recent studies (Gao et al., 2023; Chen et al., 2022) have showcased improved effectiveness in arithmetic reasoning tasks by generating Python programs that delineate the reasoning process through sequenced chained commands.

3 Methodology

3.1 Background

Logic-LM (Pan et al., 2023) is a framework to decompose a reasoning problem into three stages:

1. *Problem Formulation*, where given a task description and a problem statement LLM write symbolic formulations that represents the NL problem. In Figure 1 the NL prompt with task description is the problem formulator in Logic-LM.

2. *Symbolic Reasoning*, where we use a symbolic solver like Prover92 (Robinson, 1965)and Z3 theorem prover (Moura and Bjørner, 2008) to solve the formulations generated earlier.

3. *Result interpretation*, where the produced output is mapped to the right answer using regex parsing.

Logic-LM uses a refinement loop to fix errors in symbolic formulation at formulation and reasoning stages. However, Logic-LM still struggles to improve on logical representations, showing almost no improvement after multiple iterations. Authors attribute this to semantic limitations of the formulation. To this end, Logic-LM++ aims to mitigate this limitation by improving the Logic-LM refinement loop.

3.2 Self-Refinement Agent

Logic-LM defines the notion of a *Self-Refinement Agent* to implement the refinement loop in the symbolic formulations in cases where the formulations did not yield a successful execution within the system. This agent is characterized by a *refinement prompt* 1 PG: Add more details in figure caption. In the original work, the refinement prompt constituted various few shot examples to act as exemplar for the model. While similar techniques have proven useful (Madaan et al., 2023a; Shinn et al., 2023), we anecdotally observe that instead of helping the model it adds extra irrelevant information that distracts the model from fixing the issues relevant to the current formulation, consistent with similar studies in other domains (Pan et al., 2023). To alleviate this, instead of adding few-shots, we add the problem statement and the question to the refinement prompt alongside instructions to self-reflect on the model's failure to generate the right response. As we show later in Section 4, this structure helps better *contextualize* (Shinn et al., 2023) the formulation to the self-reflection agent and help the system generate better refinements.

3.3 Backtracking Agent

LLMs has shown remarkable results in automated evaluation benchmarks (Zheng et al., 2023b) and has shown high alignment with the human judgement (Wei et al., 2024). We use this capability of LLMs to assess if the repaired formulation by self-refinement improves the alignment of the human intent with LLM generated formulations. This allows us to get rid of the updates that are not helpful in future iterations and only use those updates where the changes help the model to come to the right formulation. In Figure 1 we can see without the backtracking agent the LLM accepts the semantically incorrect symbolic formulations as the statement "No young person teaches" is translated to "all young people teach" since the code is syntactically correct there is no proof-check on the refinement.

However, In Figure 2 we demonstrate in the same example with the backtracking agent Logic-LM++ is able to generate right formulation by us-

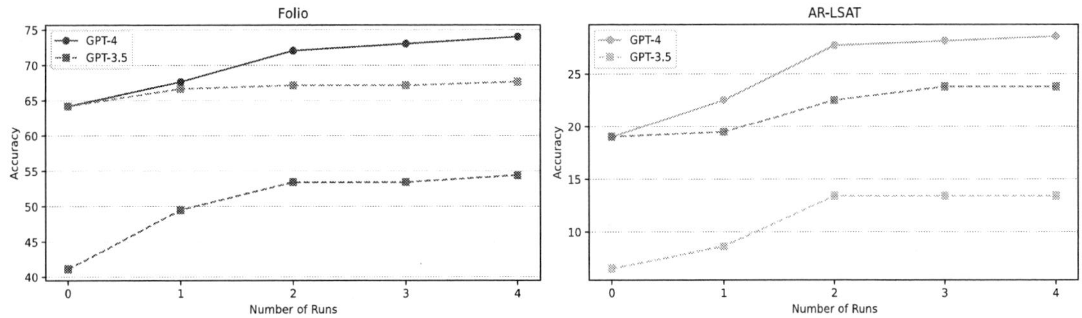

Figure 3: Accuracy in subsequent rounds of refinement. The grey line here represents the accuracy scores on self-refinement without backtracking with GPT-4.

ing the right formulation to represent "No young person teaches" and use the right formulation to describe the question "Rose is a student and Jerry is a human". This showcase how backtracking agent works as funnel to reduce the semantic error that is propagated at the refinement stage. In Figure 2 we show on comparison of the two sets of the formulation, returns a more semantically correct formulation this allows Logic-LM++ to only accept the edits if it improves or preserve the logical structure of the formulation.

		GPT-3.5 turbo		GPT-4	
BT		-	+	-	+
FOLIO	E_r	84.3	84.3	85.8	**86.7**
	E_a	64.3	**66.2**	79.9	85.8
ProofWriter	E_r	95.6	95.6	99.0	99.0
	E_a	74.1	**77.2**	79.6	79.6
AR-LSAT	E_r	21.8	**22.9**	**32.6**	32.0
	E_a	60.3	**64.1**	60.0	**66.2**

Table 2: Execution rate (E_r) and Execution Accuracy (E_a) agent with Backtracking (BT).

4 Experiments and Analysis

4.1 Dataset

FOLIO (Han et al., 2022) is a challenging expert-written dataset for logical reasoning. The problems are aligned with real-world knowledge and use natural wordings, and the questions require complex first-order logic reasoning to solve. We use the FOLIO test set for evaluation with 204 examples.

AR-LSAT (Zhong et al., 2022) is a dataset that collects all analytical logic reasoning questions from the Law School Admission Test from 1991 to 2016. We use the test set which has 231 multiple-choice questions. AR-LSAT is particularly challenging, with state-of-the-art model's performance slightly better than random guessing (Liang et al., 2022; Ribeiro et al., 2023).

ProofWriter (Tafjord et al., 2021) is another popular dataset on deductive logical reasoning. Since the problems are in more natual language like setting it makes semantic evaluation very relevant in the problem set. Logic-LM use the open-world assumption (OWA) subset in which each example is a (problem, goal) pair and the label is one of PROVED, DISPROVED, UNKNOWN. Logic-LM evaluate the pipeline with the hardest section of ProofWriter which contain total of 600 randomly sampled five step multi-hop reasoning questions.

4.2 Principal Findings

We report the final results of Logic-LM++ in Table 1. We try to answer 2 major research questions.

RQ1: Can LLMs conduct pairwise comparisons of symbolic formulations based on their relevance to a natural language task description? LLMs have demonstrated promising capabilities in pairwise comparisons for NLG evaluations (Kim et al., 2024), even in low-resource languages where their natural language generation abilities remain underdeveloped (Zheng et al., 2023a). As depicted in Table 2, the execution accuracy of the framework employing a backtracking agent is enhanced by approximately 6% with GPT-4 and around 3% with GPT3.5-turbo. Despite the average gain in execution rate being less than 1%, these statistics underscore the empirical improvements in code quality in terms of semantic correctness. Figure 1 provides a working example from the FOLIO dataset. Although the code is syntactically correct after refinement, it misinterprets a logical statement.

However, by implementing pairwise comparisons, the LLM can select the semantically correct formulation. This leads to the correct answer in the subsequent refinement iteration.

RQ2: Does refinement by LLM always positively affect the formulations?

In Figure 3, we evaluate the refinement process with and without backtracking. Logic-LM's accuracy plateaus with more runs because refined solutions may not represent the intended code. The author's also discuss this as a known limitation of the refinement process in the refinement loop they proposed. Backtracking, which reverts to the initial code if no semantic improvement is found, allows Logic-LM++ to perform consistently better by continually reassessing and correcting refinements for more reliable results.

Figure 4 shows that the backtracking agent significantly improves results in the second round within the FOLIO dataset, with a similar impact in later rounds. This indicates that backtracking is most effective early on since the generated refinement can also degrade the performance of the formulations, enabling Logic-LM++ to achieve substantial better and iterative improvements over time.

4.3 Error Analysis

Even though Logic-LM++ shows impressive improvements over standard refinement techniques, it still lacks behind in the cases where the first set of formulation generated is completely different from the ground truth formulation. On analyzing the failure cases in Logic-LM we note that the current pipeline relies a lot on fixing the bugs with current formulation without losing on semantic understanding, however in cases where the generating semantically correct formulations is hard the technique is contingent to initial formulations generated.

5 Discussion and Future Work

Figure 3 reveals a significant observation regarding the iteration increase of Logic-LM, which appears to reach convergence substantially earlier than Logic-LM++. Logic-LM associates attributes this to the hard limit of semantically correctness that can be achieved with Logic-LM. The findings stress the importance of semantic accuracy, as the Logic-LM++ exhibits consistently improved outcomes over multiple iterations, contrary to findings by Logic-LM. This outcome is primarily attributed to the model's capability to revert to the initial formulation if the refined version does not offer a semantically superior representation. Eventhough, Logic-LM++ show promising results it only focus on symbolic formulations, this effort can be well generalised to other tool augmented techniques that rely on intermediate code representation with semantic improvements during refinement.

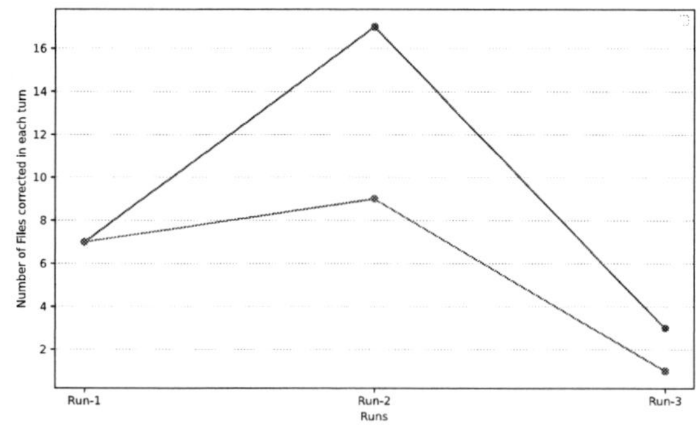

Figure 4: Number of symbolic formulations corrected after each turn of self-refinement with backtracking agent (purple) and without backtracking agent (green) in FOLIO with GPT-4.

6 Conclusion

We propose Logic-LM++ which beats state of the art results on natural language reasoning tasks on three datasets. Logic-LM++ takes leverage of LLMs' reasoning capabilities to show significant improvements in efficient use of logic solvers for reasoning, we demonstrate that LLMs show promising results at conducting comparison between symbolic formulations even in cases where generating symbolic formulations is a hard task for LLM.

Limitation

At present, Logic-LM++ faces constraints in its capacity to effectively capture the semantic intricacies in reasoning tasks. This limitation notably complicates the evaluation process, especially when dealing with smaller LLMs like (Rozière et al., 2023). The understanding required for accurate reasoning poses a significant challenge, particularly in contexts where the model's semantic comprehension may be insufficient. Due to this the assessment of performance becomes notably more complex. This limitation underscores the need for continued advancements in semantic understanding within LLMs to enhance their efficacy across reasoning tasks.

References

Tom B. Brown, Benjamin Mann, Nick Ryder, Melanie Subbiah, Jared Kaplan, Prafulla Dhariwal, Arvind Neelakantan, Pranav Shyam, Girish Sastry, Amanda Askell, Sandhini Agarwal, Ariel Herbert-Voss, Gretchen Krueger, Tom Henighan, Rewon Child, Aditya Ramesh, Daniel M. Ziegler, Jeffrey Wu, Clemens Winter, Christopher Hesse, Mark Chen, Eric Sigler, Mateusz Litwin, Scott Gray, Benjamin Chess, Jack Clark, Christopher Berner, Sam McCandlish, Alec Radford, Ilya Sutskever, and Dario Amodei. 2020. Language models are few-shot learners. In *Proceedings of the Annual Conference on Neural Information Processing Systems (NeurIPS)*.

Wenhu Chen, Xueguang Ma, Xinyi Wang, and William W. Cohen. 2022. Program of thoughts prompting: Disentangling computation from reasoning for numerical reasoning tasks. *CoRR*, abs/2211.12588.

Aakanksha Chowdhery, Sharan Narang, Jacob Devlin, Maarten Bosma, Gaurav Mishra, Adam Roberts, Paul Barham, Hyung Won Chung, Charles Sutton, Sebastian Gehrmann, et al. 2022. PaLM: Scaling Language Modeling with Pathways. *Preprint*, arXiv:2204.02311. *arXiv preprint arXiv:2204.02311*. `https://arxiv.org/abs/2204.02311`.

Karl Cobbe, Vineet Kosaraju, Mohammad Bavarian, Jacob Hilton, Reiichiro Nakano, Christopher Hesse, and John Schulman. 2021. Training verifiers to solve math word problems. *CoRR*, abs/2110.14168.

Madeline Endres, Sarah Fakhoury, Saikat Chakraborty, and Shuvendu Lahiri. 2024. Can large language models transform natural language intent into formal method postconditions? In *The ACM International Conference on the Foundations of Software Engineering (FSE)*. ACM. Https://2024.esec-fse.org/details/fse-2024-research-papers/51/Can-Large-Language-Models-Transform-Natural-Language-Intent-into-Formal-Method-Postco.

Luyu Gao, Aman Madaan, Shuyan Zhou, Uri Alon, Pengfei Liu, Yiming Yang, Jamie Callan, and Graham Neubig. 2023. PAL: program-aided language models. In *Proceedings of the International Conference on Machine Learning (ICML)*, volume 202, pages 10764–10799.

Simeng Han, Hailey Schoelkopf, Yilun Zhao, Zhenting Qi, Martin Riddell, Luke Benson, Lucy Sun, Ekaterina Zubova, Yujie Qiao, Matthew Burtell, David Peng, Jonathan Fan, Yixin Liu, Brian Wong, Malcolm Sailor, Ansong Ni, Linyong Nan, Jungo Kasai, Tao Yu, Rui Zhang, Shafiq R. Joty, Alexander R. Fabbri, Wojciech Kryscinski, Xi Victoria Lin, Caiming Xiong, and Dragomir Radev. 2022. FOLIO: natural language reasoning with first-order logic. *CoRR*, abs/2209.00840.

Shima Imani, Liang Du, and Harsh Shrivastava. 2023. Mathprompter: Mathematical reasoning using large language models. In *Proceedings of the 61st Annual Meeting of the Association for Computational Linguistics (ACL), Industry Track*, pages 37–42.

Seungone Kim, Juyoung Suk, Shayne Longpre, Bill Yuchen Lin, Jamin Shin, Sean Welleck, Graham Neubig, Moontae Lee, Kyungjae Lee, and Minjoon Seo. 2024. Prometheus 2: An open source language model specialized in evaluating other language models. *Preprint*, arXiv:2405.01535.

Takeshi Kojima, Shixiang (Shane) Gu, Machel Reid, Yutaka Matsuo, and Yusuke Iwasawa. 2022. Large language models are zero-shot reasoners. In *Advances in Neural Information Processing Systems*, volume 35, pages 22199–22213. Curran Associates, Inc.

Angeliki Lazaridou, Elena Gribovskaya, Wojciech Stokowiec, and Nikolai Grigorev. 2022. Internet-augmented language models through few-shot prompting for open-domain question answering. *CoRR*, abs/2203.05115.

Percy Liang, Rishi Bommasani, Tony Lee, Dimitris Tsipras, Dilara Soylu, Michihiro Yasunaga, Yian Zhang, Deepak Narayanan, Yuhuai Wu, Ananya Kumar, Benjamin Newman, Binhang Yuan, Bobby Yan, Ce Zhang, Christian Cosgrove, Christopher D. Manning, Christopher Ré, Diana Acosta-Navas, Drew A. Hudson, Eric Zelikman, Esin Durmus, Faisal Ladhak, Frieda Rong, Hongyu Ren, Huaxiu Yao, Jue Wang, Keshav Santhanam, Laurel J. Orr, Lucia Zheng, Mert Yüksekgönül, Mirac Suzgun, Nathan Kim, Neel Guha, Niladri S. Chatterji, Omar Khattab, Peter Henderson, Qian Huang, Ryan Chi, Sang Michael Xie, Shibani Santurkar, Surya Ganguli, Tatsunori Hashimoto, Thomas Icard, Tianyi Zhang, Vishrav Chaudhary, William Wang, Xuechen Li, Yifan Mai, Yuhui Zhang, and Yuta Koreeda. 2022. Holistic evaluation of language models. *CoRR*, abs/2211.09110.

Bo Liu, Yuqian Jiang, Xiaohan Zhang, Qiang Liu, Shiqi Zhang, Joydeep Biswas, and Peter Stone. 2023. LLM+P: empowering large language models with optimal planning proficiency. *CoRR*, abs/2304.11477.

Aman Madaan, Niket Tandon, Prakhar Gupta, Skyler Hallinan, Luyu Gao, Sarah Wiegreffe, Uri Alon, Nouha Dziri, Shrimai Prabhumoye, Yiming Yang, Shashank Gupta, Bodhisattwa Prasad Majumder, Katherine Hermann, Sean Welleck, Amir Yazdanbakhsh, and Peter Clark. 2023a. Self-refine: Iterative refinement with self-feedback. In *Advances in Neural Information Processing Systems*, volume 36, pages 46534–46594. Curran Associates, Inc.

Aman Madaan, Niket Tandon, Prakhar Gupta, Skyler Hallinan, Luyu Gao, Sarah Wiegreffe, Uri Alon, Nouha Dziri, Shrimai Prabhumoye, Yiming Yang, Shashank Gupta, Bodhisattwa Prasad Majumder, Katherine Hermann, Sean Welleck, Amir Yazdanbakhsh, and Peter Clark. 2023b. Self-refine: Iterative refinement with self-feedback. In *Advances in Neural Information Processing Systems*, volume 36, pages 46534–46594. Curran Associates, Inc.

Leonardo Mendonça de Moura and Nikolaj S. Bjørner. 2008. Z3: An efficient smt solver. In *Proceedings of the 14th International Conference of Tools and Algorithms for the Construction and Analysis of Systems (TACAS)*, volume 4963 of *Lecture Notes in Computer Science*, pages 337–340.

Reiichiro Nakano, Jacob Hilton, Suchir Balaji, Jeff Wu, Long Ouyang, Christina Kim, Christopher Hesse, Shantanu Jain, Vineet Kosaraju, William Saunders, Xu Jiang, Karl Cobbe, Tyna Eloundou, Gretchen Krueger, Kevin Button, Matthew Knight, Benjamin Chess, and John Schulman. 2021. Webgpt: Browser-assisted question-answering with human feedback. *CoRR*, abs/2112.09332.

Liangming Pan, Alon Albalak, Xinyi Wang, and William Wang. 2023. Logic-LM: Empowering large language models with symbolic solvers for faithful logical reasoning. In *Findings of the Association for Computational Linguistics: EMNLP 2023*, pages 3806–3824, Singapore. Association for Computational Linguistics.

Debjit Paul, Mete Ismayilzada, Maxime Peyrard, Beatriz Borges, Antoine Bosselut, Robert West, and Boi Faltings. 2024. Refiner: Reasoning feedback on intermediate representations. *Preprint*, arXiv:2304.01904.

Danilo Neves Ribeiro, Shen Wang, Xiaofei Ma, Henghui Zhu, Rui Dong, Deguang Kong, Juliette Burger, Anjelica Ramos, Zhiheng Huang, William Yang Wang, George Karypis, Bing Xiang, and Dan Roth. 2023. STREET: A multi-task structured reasoning and explanation benchmark. In *Proceedings of the Eleventh International Conference on Learning Representations (ICLR)*.

John Alan Robinson. 1965. A machine-oriented logic based on the resolution principle. *Journal of the ACM (JACM)*, 12(1):23–41.

Baptiste Rozière, Jonas Gehring, Fabian Gloeckle, Sten Sootla, Itai Gat, Xiaoqing Ellen Tan, Yossi Adi, Jingyu Liu, Tal Remez, Jérémy Rapin, Artyom Kozhevnikov, Ivan Evtimov, Joanna Bitton, Manish Bhatt, Cristian Canton Ferrer, Aaron Grattafiori, Wenhan Xiong, Alexandre Défossez, Jade Copet, Faisal Azhar, Hugo Touvron, Louis Martin, Nicolas Usunier, Thomas Scialom, and Gabriel Synnaeve. 2023. Code Llama: Open Foundation Models for Code. *arXiv preprint arXiv:2308.12950*.

Yongliang Shen, Kaitao Song, Xu Tan, Dongsheng Li, Weiming Lu, and Yueting Zhuang. 2023. Hugginggpt: Solving AI tasks with chatgpt and its friends in huggingface. *CoRR*, abs/2303.17580.

Weijia Shi, Sewon Min, Michihiro Yasunaga, Minjoon Seo, Rich James, Mike Lewis, Luke Zettlemoyer, and Wen-tau Yih. 2023. REPLUG: retrieval-augmented black-box language models. *CoRR*, abs/2301.12652.

Noah Shinn, Federico Cassano, Ashwin Gopinath, Karthik Narasimhan, and Shunyu Yao. 2023. Reflexion: language agents with verbal reinforcement learning. In *Advances in Neural Information Processing Systems*, volume 36, pages 8634–8652. Curran Associates, Inc.

Oyvind Tafjord, Bhavana Dalvi, and Peter Clark. 2021. ProofWriter: Generating implications, proofs, and abductive statements over natural language. In *Findings of the Association for Computational Linguistics: ACL-IJCNLP 2021*, pages 3621–3634, Online. Association for Computational Linguistics.

Xingyao Wang, Sha Li, and Heng Ji. 2022. Code4struct: Code generation for few-shot structured prediction from natural language. *CoRR*, abs/2210.12810.

Fangyun Wei, Xi Chen, and Lu Luo. 2024. Rethinking generative large language model evaluation for semantic comprehension.

Jason Wei, Xuezhi Wang, Dale Schuurmans, Maarten Bosma, brian ichter, Fei Xia, Ed Chi, Quoc V Le, and Denny Zhou. 2022. Chain-of-thought prompting elicits reasoning in large language models. In *Advances in Neural Information Processing Systems*, volume 35, pages 24824–24837. Curran Associates, Inc.

Sean Welleck, Ximing Lu, Peter West, Faeze Brahman, Tianxiao Shen, Daniel Khashabi, and Yejin Choi. 2022. Generating sequences by learning to self-correct. *Preprint*, arXiv:2211.00053.

Xi Ye, Qiaochu Chen, Isil Dillig, and Greg Durrett. 2023. Satlm: Satisfiability-aided language models using declarative prompting. In *Proceedings of NeurIPS*.

Lianmin Zheng, Wei-Lin Chiang, Ying Sheng, Siyuan Zhuang, Zhanghao Wu, Yonghao Zhuang, Zi Lin, Zhuohan Li, Dacheng Li, Eric Xing, Hao Zhang, Joseph E Gonzalez, and Ion Stoica. 2023a. Judging llm-as-a-judge with mt-bench and chatbot arena. In *Advances in Neural Information Processing Systems*, volume 36, pages 46595–46623. Curran Associates, Inc.

Lianmin Zheng, Wei-Lin Chiang, Ying Sheng, Siyuan Zhuang, Zhanghao Wu, Yonghao Zhuang, Zi Lin, Zhuohan Li, Dacheng Li, Eric Xing, Hao Zhang, Joseph E. Gonzalez, and Ion Stoica. 2023b. Judging LLM-as-a-judge with MT-bench and chatbot arena. In *Thirty-seventh Conference on Neural Information Processing Systems Datasets and Benchmarks Track*.

Wanjun Zhong, Siyuan Wang, Duyu Tang, Zenan Xu, Daya Guo, Yining Chen, Jiahai Wang, Jian Yin, Ming Zhou, and Nan Duan. 2022. Analytical reasoning of text. In *Findings of the 2022 Conference of the North American Chapter of the Association for Computational Linguistics: Human Language Technologies (NAACL-HLT)*, pages 2306–2319.

Wanjun Zhong, Siyuan Wang, Duyu Tang, Zenan Xu, Daya Guo, Jiahai Wang, Jian Yin, Ming Zhou, and

Nan Duan. 2021. AR-LSAT: investigating analytical reasoning of text. *CoRR*, abs/2104.06598.

From Good to Great: Improving Math Reasoning with Tool-Augmented Interleaf Prompting

Nuo Chen[♣] **Hongguang Li**[♢] **Baoyuan Wang**[♢] **Jia Li**[♣]

[♣]Hong Kong University of Science and Technology (Guangzhou)
Hong Kong University of Science and Technology
[♢]Xiaobing.AI
nchen022@connect.ust.hk, jialee@ust.hk

Abstract

This paper investigates the performance of Large Language Models (LLMs) and Tool-augmented LLMs in tackling complex mathematical reasoning tasks. We introduce IMR-TIP: Improving Math Reasoning with Tool-augmented Interleaf Prompting, a framework that combines the strengths of both LLMs and Tool-augmented LLMs. IMR-TIP follows the "From Good to Great" concept, collecting multiple potential solutions from both LLMs and their Tool-Augmented counterparts for the same math problem, and then selecting or re-generating the most accurate answer after cross-checking these solutions via tool-augmented interleaf prompting. The framework incorporates two key aspects: self-prompt and tool-augmented interleaf prompting (TIP). The former allows LLMs to autonomously refine and improve an initial prompt related to tool usage, while the latter enables LLMs to derive the final answer by dynamically analyzing the problem, cross-checking potential solutions, and revising previous reasoning hints in an interleaved manner. Experimental analysis shows that IMR-TIP achieves enhanced mathematical capabilities and outperforms traditional LLMs and tool-augmented LLMs in accuracy and reasoning diversity on math reasoning tasks. For instance, IMR-TIP can improve Tool-augmented ChatGPT on GSM8K-Hard from 56.0% to 65.2 %.

1 Introduction

Large language models (LLMs) (Brown et al., 2020b; Hu et al., 2021; Zeng et al., 2022; OpenAI, 2023; Chen et al., 2023a; You et al., 2022) such as GPT4 have exhibited remarkable performances across a wide array of downstream tasks. They can effortlessly tackle downstream tasks by conditioning on a scant number of in-context exemplars or plain natural language task descriptions (Brown et al., 2020a). Notwithstanding these significant advancements, even the most extensive LLMs are confronted with challenges when faced with intricate tasks that necessitate multiple reasoning steps (Gao et al., 2023; Chen et al., 2023b).

Method	Tool-Augmented LLMs			
	GSM8K	Wrong	Right	Total
LLMs-COT	Wrong	*286*	318	604
	Right	**294**	421	715
	Total	580	739	1319

Table 1: Confusion matrix between LLMs and its Tool-Augmented approach on GSM8K dataset. Here, we select the calculator as the external tool, which is implemented by `eval` function in `Python`. The experimental LLM is `text-davinci-003` (2-shot).

The capacity of LLMs to tackle complex tasks has been extensively assessed using math reasoning datasets such as GSM8K (Cobbe et al., 2021) and SVAMP (Patel et al., 2021). These datasets present math problems that cannot be directly answered but require multi-step reasoning. To encourage LLMs to engage in step-by-step reasoning, the chain-of-thought (COT) strategy (Wei et al., 2022) has emerged as the standard prompting approach. Through COT, LLMs are guided to generate a solution that consists of a sequence of intermediate steps, leading to the final answer. Nevertheless, it has been observed in previous studies that LLMs are prone to making mistakes or hallucinations, particularly during intermediate numerical computations (Qian et al., 2022; Yuan et al., 2023; Lu et al., 2022). Even a minor mistake at this stage can result in a completely incorrect final answer. In an effort to address this limitation, a series of studies (Parisi et al., 2022; Schick et al., 2023; Yao et al., 2022) have been undertaken, which leverage external tools such as the calculator to compensate for the weaknesses of LLMs. These approaches have shown significant improvements in the accuracy of answers on math reasoning tasks.

Although these approaches have led to signif-

Proceedings of the 2nd Workshop on Natural Language Reasoning and Structured Explanations (@ACL 2024), pages 64–79
August 15, 2024

icant improvements overall, a pertinent question arises: Can these tool-augmented LLMs outperform their traditional LLM-COT counterparts consistently? To explore this question, we conduct a pilot analysis at first: we test both LLMs-COT and its tool-augmented counterpart (calculator-augmented) on GSM8K dataset, separately. Table 1 meticulously compares the quantities of accurately and inaccurately predicted samples between the two methods. Upon careful analysis of the tabulated results, we can observe that incorporating a calculator has undeniably yielded a substantial boost (739 vs. 715) in the accuracy of LLMs on the GSM8K dataset. This improvement can be primarily attributed to the calculator's capability to mitigate the potential errors that could arise during mathematical computations within the model. Nevertheless, it is noteworthy that despite this tool augmentation, there persist cases (**294**) where the LLMs-COT outperforms its Tool-augmented LLMs counterpart, achieving accurate predictions where the latter faltered. Upon experimental analysis, the primary factors contributing to this phenomenon can be categorized as: 1) LLMs may generate different reasoning logic for the same math question due to the varying token sampling probabilities. 2) When employing tool-augmented LLMs to tackle math reasoning problems, stringent requirements are imposed on the output text to adhere to specific formats. For instance, calculator-augmented LLMs (Schick et al., 2023) must produce the output text in a predefined numerical equation format, ensuring seamless compatibility with the calculator's invocation. Conversely, program-augmented LLMs (Gao et al., 2023) necessitate the generation of specific code functions that can be executed effectively. These prescribed format requirements may influence the mathematical reasoning process of LLMs.

Based on the aforementioned analysis, we aim to capitalize on the strengths of both LLMs and Tool-augmented LLMs to further enhance their mathematical capabilities. In this work, we introduce **IMR-TIP**: **I**mproving **M**ath **R**easoning with **T**ool-augmented **I**nterleaf **P**rompting. IMR-TIP is a framework that follows the idea "*From Good to Great*" that first collects multiple potential solutions from LLMs and their Tool-Augmented approaches given the same math problem, and then selects the most correct answer or re-generates new answer after cross-checking these solutions in a tool-augmented interleaved manner. To achieve this, we design IMR-TIP in two aspects: (1) We first propose *self-prompt* to address the challenge of crafting clear, diverse and effective tool-based prompts. It allows LLMs to autonomously refine and improve an initial prompt related to tool usage, resulting in enhanced prompts. Moreover, the self-prompt can yield multiple diverse tool-based prompts through iterative runs without requiring repetitive manual modifications, eliciting varied reasoning paths (solutions) in LLMs. (2) Then given multiple solutions, we introduce *tool-augmented interleaf prompting* (TIP), a paradigm combining reasoning, acting, and external tools in an interleaved manner to arrive at the correct answer. TIP allows LLMs to dynamically analyze the problem, cross-check potential solutions, and re-evaluate even revising previous reasoning hints through *action* and *thought*. Our technical contributions are summarized as follows:

- We conduct an in-depth study for LLMs-COT and tool-augmented LLMs on the math reasoning tasks, make interesting observations and design a novel framework named IMR-TIP to improve LLMs.
- We introduce self-prompt to obtain diverse and machine-friendly tool-based prompts without manual effort.
- We carry out extensive experiments to verify that our proposed IMR-TIP significantly improves LLMs and their tool-augmented approaches on 5 math reasoning tasks based on two different backbones.

2 Methodology

In this section, we aim to illustrate our method in detail, as seen in Figure 1 and Figure 2. We first review the problem formulation of math problem reasoning. Then we introduce our proposed self-prompt and tool-augmented interleaf prompting methods, sequentially.

2.1 Problem formulation

A math problem solving task can be defined as $\{Q, O, A\}$, where Q is the target math question, $O = \{O_1, O_2, ..., O_k\}$ are answer options if Q is a K-way multiple choice problem, A is the corresponding ground-truth answer. Given Q and O as inputs, LLMs can directly output answers or output a sequence of tokens as intermediate reasoning

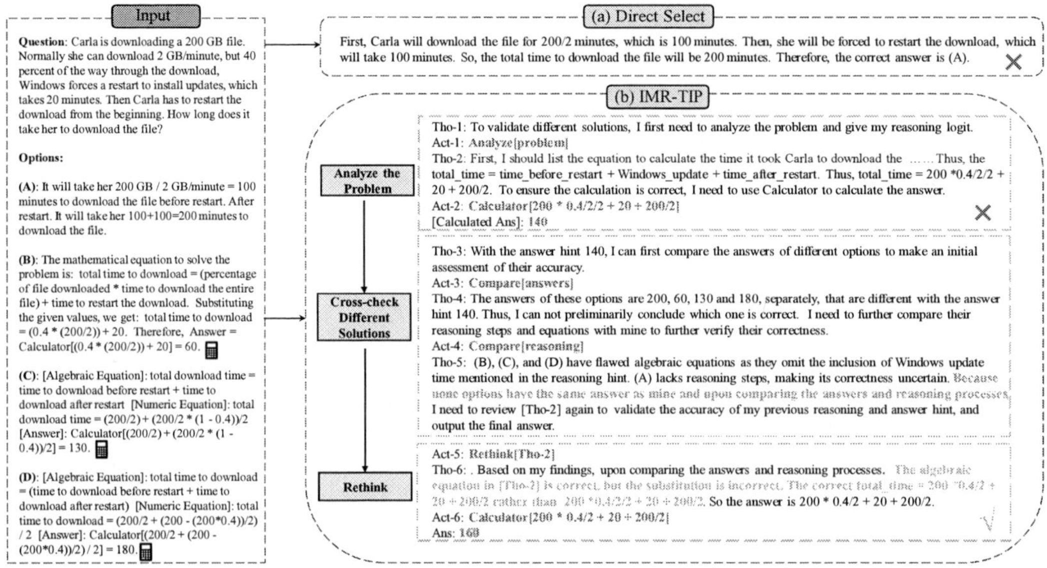

Figure 1: Comparison of 2 prompting methods: (a) *Direct Select*, which requires LLMs to select the correct one from options. (b) IMR-TIP, which derives the correct answer in an interleaved manner with *action* and *thought*. In this example, we present 3 options (Option B, C, D) from tool-augmented LLMs (using the calculator) and 1 option from LLMs COT (Option A). Tho and Act are short for Thought and Action, respectively.

steps R via COT. Then we can obtain the answer in R through regular expression matching.

2.2 IMR-TIP

The key insights of the proposed methods are twofold: (1) We first propose self-prompt to obtain diverse tool-based prompts to induce more diverse reasoning paths and solutions. (2) We then introduce TIP to better derive the final answer from multiple reasoning solutions from LLMs and tool-augmented LLMs. The flow of our TIP can be defined as: **Initial answer determination from question analysis $\rightarrow$ Cross-Validation of options accuracy $\rightarrow$ Further verification of reasoning if discrepancies arise $\rightarrow$ Rethinking for answer accuracy if uncertain $\rightarrow$ Final answer**.

2.2.1 Self-Prompt

Crafting clear, diverse and concise tool-based prompts, which encompasses the output format, tool definition, and usage instructions, proves more challenging than traditional COT. Thus, we propose self-prompt to address this issue. Moreover, different from previous works (Wang et al., 2022; Li et al., 2023) that focus on generating k reasoning paths from one fixed prompt by sampling decoding, which limits the diversity of reasoning paths. Our proposed self-prompt can produce diverse prompts, automatically increasing prompt diversity and encouraging LLMs to think differently, eliminating the need for repetitive manual writing and editing. Concretely, we design self-prompt in three steps, as shown in Figure 2:

- Step1: We first give an initial tool-based prompt to the LLM with the instruction: "Summary the drawbacks of the current prompt and give some advice".
- Step2: With the advice and prompt problems that are outputted from LLMs, we then instruct the LLM with: "According to your advice, please rewrite the current prompt". Thus, the LLM can output the revised prompt.
- Step3: Given the revised prompt as input and ask the LLM: "Is there any problem with the revised prompt?". If the LLM responds "Yes" we will repeat steps 1 to 3 until the LLM answers "No". Otherwise, this is the final improved prompt.

Overall, our self-prompt follows the idea that "LLMs know themselves better". Through the steps mentioned above, we not only address the issue of manually crafting reasonable and clear instructions for LLMs to use tools but also enhance the diversity of prompts simultaneously via running self-prompt through multiple iterations. Experimentally, the improved tool-based prompt can help LLMs achieve better performances compared with the initial prompt. We can run it M times, resulting

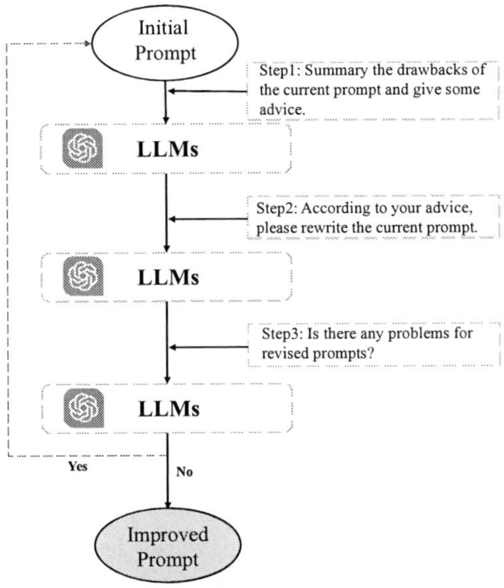

Figure 2: Overview of self-prompt.

in M diverse prompts, and then sample N reasoning paths for each prompt via sampling decoding. This way, we can obtain K = M × N tool-based diverse reasoning paths for each math problem.

2.2.2 Tool-augmented Interleaf Prompting

The core idea of TIP is: We augment the reasoning paths for each question from 1 to K+L, where L from LLMs [1] and K from their tool-augmented LLMs (obtained from self-prompt). Then we derive the final answer by observing and validating these solutions (reasoning paths) in an interleaved manner, which can be formalized as $\mathcal{TIP}(\hat{A}|Q, R_1, ...R_{K+L})$. TIP is similar to how a human brain learns when solving mathematical and multiple-choice questions: given a question and different possible solutions, analyze the problem, observe the solutions to find how the question should be solved, and then learn from these solutions, memorize or revise its own solution, conclude the answer at last.

Following this, We decompose TIP into three major steps. Given a question and multiple potential solutions: (1) ANALYZE THE PROBLEM: Before validating different answers, LLMs first need to analyze the problem and give their own reasoning logical via generating algebraic and numerical expression; (2) CROSS-CHECK DIFFERENT SOLUTIONS: Then based on the above reasoning hint, LLMs can cross-check different solutions. Considering LLMs could occasionally conclude accurate answers when generating wrong reasoning paths, we break down this into two sub-steps: compare the numerical answers and then cross-verify intermediate steps, which explores whether each solution is both sound and accurate. (3) RETHINK: Unlike traditional multiple-choice question answering tasks, where there is at least one correct solution and reliable reasoning hints, in our case, all four solutions could be incorrect, and previous reasoning hints might also be flawed. Hence, we introduce an extra step called "Rethink" which requires LLMs to review and correct their initial answer hints after observing and checking different solutions, outputting the final answer. We argue that LLMs are capable of gaining a deeper understanding of the problem by cross-checking various solutions.

Inspired by ReAct (Yao et al., 2022), we let LLMs achieve each step in an interleaved manner with *thought* and *action*. In each step, LLM receives the environmental context c_t and takes an action $a_t \in \mathcal{A}$, where $c_t = \{t_1, a_1, ..., t_{t-1}, a_{t-1}\}$ and $\mathcal{A}$ is the action space. t_1, a_1 are previous *thought* and *action* at step 1. As shown in Figure 1, there could be multiple types of useful *thoughts*, like creating action plans (*Tho-1*), reasoning process of executing the action (*Tho-2*), reasoning over the context (*Tho-6*).

Action Space As we focus on math reasoning tasks, $\mathcal{A}$ consists of the following actions to support interactive TIP: (1) *Analyze[]*, which requires analyzing the specific solution or the math problem. (2) *Compare[]*, which requires comparing and cross-checking answers or intermediate steps from different solutions or the generated answer hints. (3) *Rethink[]*, which means to double-check or review the specific thinking process in previous *thoughts*. (4) *Calculator[]*, which calls the calculator to compute the expression.

Figure 1 shows a typical example of IMR-TIP. In this example, all options are the wrong solutions, and the *direct select* and *self-consistency* approaches also give the wrong answers. In our proposed IMR-TIP, despite making an initial error in predicting during the "analyze the problem" step, the model self-corrects by cross-checking and identifying the correct equation formulation in the *Tho-2*, albeit with an algebraic mistake. In the *Tho-6*, it rectifies the error, resulting in the correct answer via calling the calculator.

Overall, our IMR-TIP has the following salient

[1] In our experiments, we obtain L reasoning paths from LLMs by sampling decoding.

features for solving math reasoning tasks: (I) Multi-view Reasoning paths: Approaching the math problem from multiple perspectives from LLMs and tool-augmented LLMs; (II) Multi-verification: Comparing and cross-checking the different solutions to a reasoning hint, including verifying the correctness of numeric answers and the intermediate steps, aiming at providing a more accurate understanding of the problem; (III) Calculation-Verification: Using the calculator to calculate the expression or verify the result; (IV) Self-Check: Re-checking the reasoning paths that include algebraic equation and substitution in previous reasoning hints after cross-checking different solutions.

In theory, M, N, K and L could be assigned higher values, resulting in more reasoning paths. However, due to the fact that these K+L solutions will be subsequently used as inputs for our TIP, we must take into account the *limitations posed by input token length and associated costs* in the in-context learning setting. Experimentally, we have determined that setting M=3, N=1, K = M $\times$ N =3 and L=1 is appropriate.

3 Experiments

In this section, we first review our testing datasets and evaluation metrics. Then we briefly introduce our experimental settings that include backbones, and our prompts. At last, we will present our main results and ablation studies.

3.1 Datasets and Metrics

Datasets We validate our proposed approach on five math reasoning datasets: (1) **MAWPS** (Koncel-Kedziorski et al., 2016) serves as a collection of math word problems (MWPs), offering a unified testbed with 1921 samples for accessing various algorithms. (2) **SVAMP** (Patel et al., 2021), short for Simple Variations on Arithmetic Math Word Problems, is an elementary-level MWP dataset that contains 1000 examples in test set. (3) **GSM8K** (Cobbe et al., 2021) stands as a dataset comprising 1391 linguistically diverse grade school MWPs, meticulously crafted by human problem writers to ensure high quality. (4) **GSM8K-Hard** (Gao et al., 2023), an advanced iteration of GSM8K, which substitutes numbers in the questions with larger counterparts. This modification aims to assess the generalization capability of LLMs when dealing with substantial numerical values. (5) Given the limited range of three-digit numbers in the SVAMP dataset, we enhanced model assessment by randomly replacing query numbers with values between 100,000 and 10,000,000. This adjustment, while maintaining original reasoning logic, lead to the creation of **SVAMP-Hard**. SVAMP-Hard and GSM8K-Hard provide a more rigorous test of LLMs' mathematical computational capabilities.

Metrics Following previous standard works, we use the **Accuracy** as the evaluation metrics.

3.2 Experimental Settings

Backbone We conduct our experiments based on two OpenAI LLMs: GPT-3 (`text-davinci-003`) and GPT-3.5 (`gpt-3.5-turbo`) through Azure Service. We use the default parameters except temperature = 0 for greedy decoding during inference. In our experiments, we select the calculator as the external tool for tool-augmented approaches, which is implemented by Python *eval()* function.

Exemplars All quintet mathematical reasoning datasets allocate two exemplars, which are arbitrarily selected solely from the GSM8K-trainset, for both LLMs-COT and tool-enhanced LLMs. In TIP, we manually compose trajectories to use three exemplars in the prompts. Each trajectory includes multiple thought-action steps, where each thought is free-form. LLMs combine these thoughts to devise a plan ("... I first need to analyze x"), guide the reasoning process ("Option (A) is right, I then ..."), call tool ("use the calculator to compute y"), and conclude the answer ("the answer is z"). The model will end with "[Ans]" when solving the task. See Appendix A for more details about LLMs-COT, tool-augmented LLMs and TIP prompts.

Baselines We mainly compare our approach with the following baselines: (1) **COT**, which solves the problem via step-by-step reasoning with our own implementations. (2) **Tool-Augmented**, signifies LLMs employing calculators for expression computation with *initial tool-based prompts*, as elucidated in preceding sections. In this way, LLMs always need to follow a specific output format. (4) **Self-Prompt**, which utilizes the *improved too-based prompts* from self-prompt to solve math reasoning tasks. (5) **Toolformer** (Schick et al., 2023), a sophisticated paradigm that enables language models like GPT-J to utilize external tools, optimizing their performance in various tasks through fine-tuning. (4) **ART** (Paranjape et al., 2023), a framework facilitating automatic multi-step reasoning and tool-use

Backbone	Algorithms	Dataset					
		MAWPS	SVAMP	SVAMP-H	GSM8K	GSM8K-H	Average
GPT-J	Toolformer	44.0	29.4	-	-	-	-
GPT-3 (text-davinci-003)	ART	90.1	76.2	-	-	-	-
	COT	89.6	77.1	29.5	54.2	20.4	54.2
	Tool-Augmented	89.9	77.6	69.9	55.5	44.1	67.3
	Self-Prompt	90.1	78.5	70.0	56.1	44.5	67.8
	IMR-TIP	**90.7**	**79.3**	**73.7**	**61.5**	**47.4**	**70.5**
GPT-3.5 (gpt-3.5-turbo)	COT	91.0	76.5	39.2	73.0	35.0	62.9
	Tool-Augmented	91.9	77.0	78.5	75.5	54.0	75.4
	Self-Prompt	92.1	78.0	79.7	76.0	56.0	76.4
	IMR-TIP	**92.6**	**79.3**	**82.0**	**79.1**	**65.2**	**79.6**

Table 2: The overall results on the five datasets. We highlight the best results for each backbone. In our experiments, as we obtain 3 improved tool-based prompts through self-prompt (Section 3), we report their average results. SVAMP-H and GSM8K-H are short for SVAMP-Hard and GSM8K-Hard. We report average results of 3 runs.

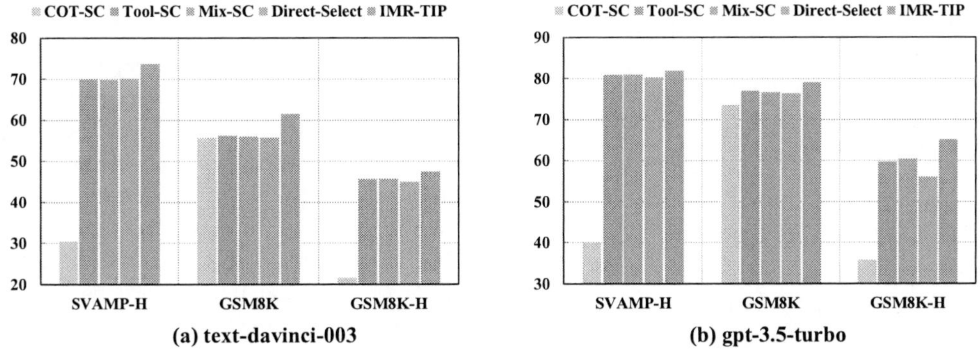

Figure 3: Ablation studies of different prompting methods based on `text-davinci-003` and `gpt-3.5-turbo`.

Models	SVAMP-H	GSM8K	GSM8K-H
IMR-TIP	**73.7**	**61.5**	**47.4**
w/ Step-I	70.4	56.3	44.5
w/ Step-II	72.4	58.7	45.6
w/ Step-I + II	72.9	59.4	46.5

Table 3: Ablation studies in our IMR-TIP. Here, we conduct results based on `text-davinci-003`.

integration for LLMs.

For ablations, we also compare ours with (1) *Self-consistency*: We build self-consistency baselines based on LLMs and their tool-augmented counterparts, named **COT-SC** and **Tool-SC**, separately. For a fair comparison, we sample reasoning paths 3 times by setting the temperature as 0.7. Then we also introduce **Mix-SC**, which votes the most consistent answer from the given solutions in TIP as the prediction. (2) *Direct Select*: Given a math problem, multiple solutions from LLMs and tool-augmented LLMs, we regard it as a multiple choice question answering task and require LLMs directly selecting one of them as the answer through COT. We show an example of it in Figure 1. See Appendix A for more details about their definitions.

Of note, although other works, such as PAL (Gao et al., 2023), employs tools like programming languages for math problem-solving, we do not compare our method with theirs in this paper to maintain fairness, as our tools differ.

3.3 Main Results

Table 2 shows the results of three backbone models with various prompting algorithms. Some key observations are as follows from the table:

LLMs still suffer in math calculations. It is evident that the performances of these two backbone LLMs with COT on SVAMP-Hard and GSM8K-Hard are notably lower compared to their performance on SVAMP and GSM8K (e.g., 77.1% vs.29.5% on SVAMP and SVAMP-Hard). This discrepancy suggests that when tasked with computations involving larger numerical values, these LLMs exhibit an increased susceptibility to calculation errors. Interestingly, GPT-3.5 shows better computation ability than GPT-3.

Self-prompt benefits the performances for tool-using. Across all datasets, it is discernible that the prompts subjected to self-prompt adjustments manifest enhanced performance relative to their original counterparts. This enhancement is attributed to the provision of more lucid and explicit tool usage instructions, alongside a heightened standardization of input-output formats.

IMR-TIP outperforms other baselines consistently, particularly on more challenging datasets involving complex computations. Firstly, the table highlights the tool-augmented method's superiority over the traditional COT approach on all datasets, attributed to enhanced computational abilities. Secondly, our approach yields additional enhancements across all datasets, notably pronounced in the more challenging SVAMP-Hard and GSM8K-Hard sets demanding higher computational prowess. For example, IMR-TIP based on GPT-3.5 could improve COT and Self-Prompt from 35.0%, 56.0% to 65.2% on GSM8K-Hard.

3.4 Ablation Study

In this part, we conduct ablation studies to verify the impact of (1) each key component in IMR-TIP; (2) self-prompt (**How well prompts from self-prompt perform specifically?** See Appendix B for more details.).

Key Components Given the sequential nature of our three-step IMP process (See Section 3), our ablation study comprises three sub-experiments in Table 3: 1) Step I only; 2) Step II only; 3) Steps I and II together. Table 3 shows that: 1. Step II holds paramount importance; 2. Steps I and III also exhibit significance; 3. The combined use of all three steps yields optimal performance.

4 Analysis

IMR-TIP vs. Self-consistency Given multiple solutions from LLMs and tool-augmented LLMs, two intuitive ways to derive the answer are: 1) *Self-Consistency*; 2) *Direct Select*. As aforementioned, we have three versions of self-consistency: COT-SC, Tool-SC and Mix-SC. Figure 3 shows the comparison between ours and these approaches on three datasets. We can observe that Tool-SC and Mix-SC perform comparably but they perform much better than COT-SC, just as tool-augmented LLMs surpass LLM-COT. Across two distinct backbone models, IMR-TIP consistently outperforms other methods on each dataset.

4.1 Why IMR-TIP works?

In pursuit of a comprehensive dissection of our IMR-TIP's underlying mechanics, we proffer a distributional analysis capturing the trajectory through which IMR-TIP reaches its definitive answers. Table 5 delineates the proportions in which IMR-TIP either selects answers from provided options or re-generates new answers on SVAMP-Hard and GSM8K-Hard datasets. The former is segmented into three categories of assessment by IMR-TIP: solely based on LLM's answer, based on both the LLM and the Tool-augmented methods, and exclusively within the Tool-augmented method. Predominantly, IMR-TIP favors answers from Tool-augmented LLMs that are derived from provided solutions. Notably, IMR-TIP's capacity for generating new answers through observation and cross-checking significantly enhances its performance relative to self-consistency. This unique capability distinguishes IMR-TIP from other methods.

We remain curious about the performance of IMR-TIP when not all the given options are necessarily correct. To verify this, we conduct in-depth analysis of the GSM8K-Hard dataset in Table 6 shows that our model incorrectly answers 2.7% of cases when all provided answer choices are correct. Conversely, it correctly answers 5.2% of cases when all choices are incorrect. These outcomes highlight the challenges in enabling a model to self-verify and self-correct. Despite some errors, **our method strengthens LLM's ability to enhance its understanding and correct mistakes through interleaving reasoning steps**, which is a central aspect of our approach.

Case Study Table 4 shows the an example from IMR-TIP and self-consistency on the GSM8K dataset. In this instance, only option (D) stands correct, with option (A) exhibiting a computational error, and both options (B) and (C) featuring accurate algebraic expressions albeit flawed numerical substitutions. Within this context, Mix-SC would favor the most consistently occurring answer, leading to the selection of 44 as the predicted answer, despite its inaccuracy. While our approach also encounters numerical substitution errors in [Tho-2], meticulous scrutiny of both the answer and reasoning steps reveals the preceding mistake, affirming the correctness of option (D). This case underscores another inherent advantage of IMR-TIP over self-consistency: the capacity to derive an accurate answer through thoughtful reasoning, rather than a

Question: Sadie slept 8 hours on Monday. For next two days, she slept 2 hours less, each, because she had to complete some assignments. If the rest of the week she slept 1 hour more than those two days, how many hours did she sleep in total throughout the week?
(A): Sadie slept 8 hours on Monday. For the next two days, she slept 2 hours less, each, so she slept 6 hours each day. If the rest of the week she slept 1 hour more than those two days, she slept 7 hours each day. So the total amount of hours she slept throughout the week is 8+6+6+7+7+7+7=42. So the answer is 42.
(B): The mathematical equation to solve the problem is: total hours slept = (Monday's hours + (2 days * (hours - 2)) + (4 days * (hours + 1))). Substituting the given values, we get: total hours slept = (8 + (2 * (6 - 2)) + (4 * (6 + 1))). Therefore, Answer = Calculator[8 + (2 * (6 - 2)) + (4 * (6 + 1))] = 44.
(C): [Algebraic Equation]: Total hours slept = (Monday's hours + (2 days * (Monday's hours - 2 hours)) + (4 days * (Monday's hours - 2 hours + 1 hour)) [Numeric Equation]: Total hours slept = (8 + (2 * (8 - 2)) + (4 * (8 - 2))) [Answer]: Calculator[(8 + (2 * (8 - 2)) + (4 * (8 - 2)))] = 44.
(D): [Algebraic Equation]: total hours slept = hours slept on Monday + (hours slept on Tuesday + hours slept on Wednesday + hours slept on Thursday + hours slept on Friday + hours slept on Saturday + hours slept on Sunday) [Numeric Equation]: total hours slept = 8 + (6 + 6 + 7 + 7 + 7 + 7) [Answer]: Calculator[8 + (6 + 6 + 7 + 7 + 7 + 7)] = 48.

IMR-TIP:
Tho-1: To validate different solutions, I first need to analyze the math problem and give my reasoning logic.
Act-1: ***Analyze[problem]***
Tho-2: I need to find the total amount of hours Sadie slept throughout the week given the information that she slept 8 hours on Monday, 2 hours less for the next two days, and 1 hour more for the rest of the week. Thus, the total hours = 8 + (2 * (8 - 2)) + (4 * (8 - 2)). To ensure the calculation is correct, I need to use Calculator to calculate the answer.
Act-2: Calculator[8 + (2 * (8 - 2)) + (4 * (8 - 2))]
Tho-3: With the answer hint 44, I can first compare their answers to make an initial assessment of their accuracy.
Act-3: ***Compare[answers]***
Tho-4: I observe that (A) directly gives the answer while (B), (C) and (D) use the Calculator to compute the answer. The answers of them are 42, 44, 44, 48. Half of them align with the answer hint 44, I can preliminarily conclude that (B), (C) are correct. But there are still two different answers, I cannot determine which answer is definitely correct. Thus, I can compare their reasoning steps and equations with mine to further verify their correctness.
Act-4: ***Compare[reasoning]***
Tho-5: (A) and (D) follow similar reasoning paths and their mathematical equations are the same, but their answers are different. Due to (D) using the calculator, (A) must have mistakes in calculation. (B) and (C) give similar algebraic equations, but their substitutions are incorrect. (B) states that Sadie slept 6 hours each day for the next two days, which is not accurate. (C) is also incorrect. I may also make a mistake in [Tho-2] because my numerical equation is the same as (C). I need to review [Tho-2] again to validate the accuracy of my previous reasoning and answer hint.
Act-5: ***Rethink[Tho-2]***.
Tho-6: Based on my findings, the algebraic equation in [Tho-2] is correct, but the substitution is incorrect. The correct total hours = 8 + (2 * (8 - 2)) + (4 * (8 - 2 + 1)) rather than 8 + (2 * (8 - 2)) + (4 * (8 - 2)).
Act-6: Calculator[8 + (2 * (8 - 2)) + (4 * (8 - 2 + 1))]
Tho-7: After revising the substitution in [Tho-2], I think the final answer is 48 and (D) is correct.
Ans: **48**

Mix-SC: 44.

Table 4: Examples of generated solutions by IMR-TIP and self-consistency on GSM8K dataset.

	Answer Type	SVAMP-H	GSM8K-H
Select	Only LLM	4.5%	6.3%
	LLM and Tool	13.4%	18.5%
	Only Tool	79.0%	67.1%
Re-generate new answers		3.1%	8.1%

Table 5: Proportion of each answer type in our IMR-TIP. Here, we conduct results based on `gpt-3.5-turbo`.

Method	Answer options have the right answer?			
	GSM8K-H (%)	Yes	No	Total
IMR-TIP	Wrong	**2.7%**	31.8%	34.5%
	Right	60.3%	**5.2%**	65.5%
	Total	63.0%	37.0%	100%

Table 6: Ours performance when provided with answer choices that are either correct or incorrect in GSM8K-Hard dataset. The experimental LLMs is `gpt-3.5-turbo`.

simplistic reliance on majority voting for consistency. We present more cases in Appendix C.

5 Conclusion

This work introduces IMR-TIP, a framework designed to capitalize on the strengths of both conventional and tool-augmented LLMs, enhancing their mathematical capabilities. IMR-TIP employs self-prompt to refine its initial prompts. Additionally, it utilizes tool-augmented interleaf prompting (TIP) to reach the correct answer. This process involves interleaved *Action* and *Thought*, which encompasses analyzing the problem, observing, cross-verifying different solutions, and even rethinking previous answer hints. Through rigorous experimentation and comprehensive analysis of math reasoning tasks, IMR-TIP demonstrates a substantial enhancement over established baselines.

Limitations

In our study on enhancing the mathematical capabilities of Large Language Models (LLMs) through prompt engineering, we acknowledge two primary limitations: the potential for inaccuracies and the concern over prompt length. Despite the method's promising results, it is susceptible to errors in specific scenarios, which may affect the model's overall reliability. Moreover, the use of extended prompts, while instrumental in our approach, introduces practical constraints related to processing time and model usability. Recognizing these challenges, future research will focus on developing training techniques aimed at improving the LLM's self-revision abilities and optimizing prompt length. This direction is expected to mitigate current limitations and further the application of LLMs in complex problem-solving tasks.

References

Tom Brown, Benjamin Mann, Nick Ryder, Melanie Subbiah, Jared D Kaplan, Prafulla Dhariwal, Arvind Neelakantan, Pranav Shyam, Girish Sastry, Amanda Askell, et al. 2020a. Language models are few-shot learners. *Advances in neural information processing systems*, 33:1877–1901.

Tom B. Brown, Benjamin Mann, Nick Ryder, Melanie Subbiah, Jared Kaplan, Prafulla Dhariwal, Arvind Neelakantan, Pranav Shyam, Girish Sastry, Amanda Askell, Sandhini Agarwal, Ariel Herbert-Voss, Gretchen Krueger, Tom Henighan, Rewon Child, Aditya Ramesh, Daniel M. Ziegler, Jeffrey Wu, Clemens Winter, Christopher Hesse, Mark Chen, Eric Sigler, Mateusz Litwin, Scott Gray, Benjamin Chess, Jack Clark, Christopher Berner, Sam McCandlish, Alec Radford, Ilya Sutskever, and Dario Amodei. 2020b. Language models are few-shot learners. *CoRR*, abs/2005.14165.

Nuo Chen, Hongguang Li, Yinan Bao, Junqing He, Xinshi Lin, Qi Yang, Jianfeng Liu, Ruyi Gan, Jiaxing Zhang, Baoyuan Wang, et al. 2023a. Orca: A few-shot benchmark for chinese conversational machine reading comprehension. *arXiv preprint arXiv:2302.13619*.

Nuo Chen, Zinan Zheng, Ning Wu, Linjun Shou, Ming Gong, Yangqiu Song, Dongmei Zhang, and Jia Li. 2023b. Breaking language barriers in multilingual mathematical reasoning: Insights and observations. *arXiv preprint arXiv:2310.20246*.

Wenhu Chen, Xueguang Ma, Xinyi Wang, and William W Cohen. 2022. Program of thoughts prompting: Disentangling computation from reasoning for numerical reasoning tasks. *arXiv preprint arXiv:2211.12588*.

Karl Cobbe, Vineet Kosaraju, Mohammad Bavarian, Mark Chen, Heewoo Jun, Lukasz Kaiser, Matthias Plappert, Jerry Tworek, Jacob Hilton, Reiichiro Nakano, Christopher Hesse, and John Schulman. 2021. Training verifiers to solve math word problems. *CoRR*, abs/2110.14168.

Luyu Gao, Aman Madaan, Shuyan Zhou, Uri Alon, Pengfei Liu, Yiming Yang, Jamie Callan, and Graham Neubig. 2023. Pal: Program-aided language models. In *International Conference on Machine Learning*, pages 10764–10799. PMLR.

Zhibin Gou, Zhihong Shao, Yeyun Gong, Yujiu Yang, Minlie Huang, Nan Duan, Weizhu Chen, et al. 2023. Tora: A tool-integrated reasoning agent for mathematical problem solving. *arXiv preprint arXiv:2309.17452*.

Edward J Hu, Yelong Shen, Phillip Wallis, Zeyuan Allen-Zhu, Yuanzhi Li, Shean Wang, Lu Wang, and Weizhu Chen. 2021. Lora: Low-rank adaptation of large language models. *arXiv preprint arXiv:2106.09685*.

Shima Imani, Liang Du, and Harsh Shrivastava. 2023. Mathprompter: Mathematical reasoning using large language models. In *ACL (industry)*, pages 37–42. Association for Computational Linguistics.

Rik Koncel-Kedziorski, Subhro Roy, Aida Amini, Nate Kushman, and Hannaneh Hajishirzi. 2016. MAWPS: A math word problem repository. In *Proceedings of the 2016 Conference of the North American Chapter of the Association for Computational Linguistics: Human Language Technologies*, pages 1152–1157, San Diego, California. Association for Computational Linguistics.

Yifei Li, Zeqi Lin, Shizhuo Zhang, Qiang Fu, Bei Chen, Jian-Guang Lou, and Weizhu Chen. 2023. Making language models better reasoners with step-aware verifier. In *Proceedings of the 61st Annual Meeting of the Association for Computational Linguistics (Volume 1: Long Papers)*, pages 5315–5333.

Pan Lu, Liang Qiu, Wenhao Yu, Sean Welleck, and Kai-Wei Chang. 2022. A survey of deep learning for mathematical reasoning. *arXiv preprint arXiv:2212.10535*.

Qing Lyu, Shreya Havaldar, Adam Stein, Li Zhang, Delip Rao, Eric Wong, Marianna Apidianaki, and Chris Callison-Burch. 2023. Faithful chain-of-thought reasoning. *arXiv preprint arXiv:2301.13379*.

OpenAI. 2023. Gpt-4 technical report.

Bhargavi Paranjape, Scott Lundberg, Sameer Singh, Hannaneh Hajishirzi, Luke Zettlemoyer, and Marco Tulio Ribeiro. 2023. Art: Automatic multi-step reasoning and tool-use for large language models. *arXiv preprint arXiv:2303.09014*.

Aaron Parisi, Yao Zhao, and Noah Fiedel. 2022. Talm: Tool augmented language models. *arXiv preprint arXiv:2205.12255*.

Arkil Patel, Satwik Bhattamishra, and Navin Goyal. 2021. Are NLP models really able to solve simple math word problems? In *Proceedings of the 2021 Conference of the North American Chapter of the Association for Computational Linguistics: Human Language Technologies*, pages 2080–2094, Online. Association for Computational Linguistics.

Jing Qian, Hong Wang, Zekun Li, Shiyang Li, and Xifeng Yan. 2022. Limitations of language models in arithmetic and symbolic induction. *arXiv preprint arXiv:2208.05051*.

Teven Le Scao, Angela Fan, Christopher Akiki, Ellie Pavlick, Suzana Ilić, Daniel Hesslow, Roman Castagné, Alexandra Sasha Luccioni, François Yvon, Matthias Gallé, et al. 2022. Bloom: A 176b-parameter open-access multilingual language model. *arXiv preprint arXiv:2211.05100*.

Timo Schick, Jane Dwivedi-Yu, Roberto Dessì, Roberta Raileanu, Maria Lomeli, Luke Zettlemoyer, Nicola Cancedda, and Thomas Scialom. 2023. Toolformer: Language models can teach themselves to use tools. *arXiv preprint arXiv:2302.04761*.

Xuezhi Wang, Jason Wei, Dale Schuurmans, Quoc Le, Ed Chi, Sharan Narang, Aakanksha Chowdhery, and Denny Zhou. 2022. Self-consistency improves chain of thought reasoning in language models. *arXiv preprint arXiv:2203.11171*.

Jason Wei, Xuezhi Wang, Dale Schuurmans, Maarten Bosma, Fei Xia, Ed Chi, Quoc V Le, Denny Zhou, et al. 2022. Chain-of-thought prompting elicits reasoning in large language models. *Advances in Neural Information Processing Systems*, 35:24824–24837.

Yixuan Weng, Minjun Zhu, Shizhu He, Kang Liu, and Jun Zhao. 2022. Large language models are reasoners with self-verification. *arXiv preprint arXiv:2212.09561*.

Shunyu Yao, Jeffrey Zhao, Dian Yu, Nan Du, Izhak Shafran, Karthik Narasimhan, and Yuan Cao. 2022. React: Synergizing reasoning and acting in language models. *arXiv preprint arXiv:2210.03629*.

Chenyu You, Nuo Chen, Fenglin Liu, Shen Ge, Xian Wu, and Yuexian Zou. 2022. End-to-end spoken conversational question answering: Task, dataset and model. In *Findings of the Association for Computational Linguistics: NAACL 2022*, pages 1219–1232, Seattle, United States. Association for Computational Linguistics.

Zheng Yuan, Hongyi Yuan, Chuanqi Tan, Wei Wang, and Songfang Huang. 2023. How well do large language models perform in arithmetic tasks? *arXiv preprint arXiv:2304.02015*.

Aohan Zeng, Xiao Liu, Zhengxiao Du, Zihan Wang, Hanyu Lai, Ming Ding, Zhuoyi Yang, Yifan Xu, Wendi Zheng, Xiao Xia, et al. 2022. Glm-130b: An open bilingual pre-trained model. *arXiv preprint arXiv:2210.02414*.

Denny Zhou, Nathanael Schärli, Le Hou, Jason Wei, Nathan Scales, Xuezhi Wang, Dale Schuurmans, Claire Cui, Olivier Bousquet, Quoc Le, et al. 2022. Least-to-most prompting enables complex reasoning in large language models. *arXiv preprint arXiv:2205.10625*.

A Related Work

Math Reasoning with LLMs In recent times, large language models (LLMs) have demonstrated remarkable abilities in handling complex reasoning tasks (Scao et al., 2022; Cobbe et al., 2021; Zhou et al., 2022; Weng et al., 2022; Chen et al., 2023b; Gou et al., 2023). Rather than providing direct final answers as outputs, prior research has shown that by employing diverse prompting methods such as Chain-of-Thought (COT) prompting (Wei et al., 2022), LLMs can be guided through step-by-step reasoning, resulting in notably improved performance across a wide array of reasoning tasks. Imani et al. (2023) propose to generate multiple algebraic expressions or Python functions to solve the same math problem, aiming to explore different potential solutions. Li et al. (2023) introduce a step-aware verifier to check the reasoning steps in COT, improving the reasoning capabilities. Self-Consistency (Wang et al., 2022) is another effective work that combines different solutions and gets a final answer by aggregating to retrieve the most consistent answer. Among them, self-consistency bears resemblance to our proposed TIP, but our main distinction lies in the following: Given several solutions, our TIP can re-generate a new answer after cross-validating these solutions. In contrast, self-consistency can only select the most consistent answer from the existing ones.

Tool-Augmented LLMs Currently, researchers have undertaken a wide array of studies aimed at enriching the step-by-step reasoning process. These approaches include investigating the utilization of external tools (Parisi et al., 2022; Schick et al., 2023; Yao et al., 2022), like program interpreters (Lyu et al., 2023; Chen et al., 2022) and the calculator (Schick et al., 2023), training and utilizing external reasoning modules. For example, ReAct (Yao et al., 2022) proposes an interleaved framework with utilizing an external search engine to solve multi-hop question answering tasks. More recently, Toolformer (Schick et al., 2023) introduces a pipeline for training LLMs that can call tools during training and inference. Parallel to these works, our work can be seen as a preliminary ex-

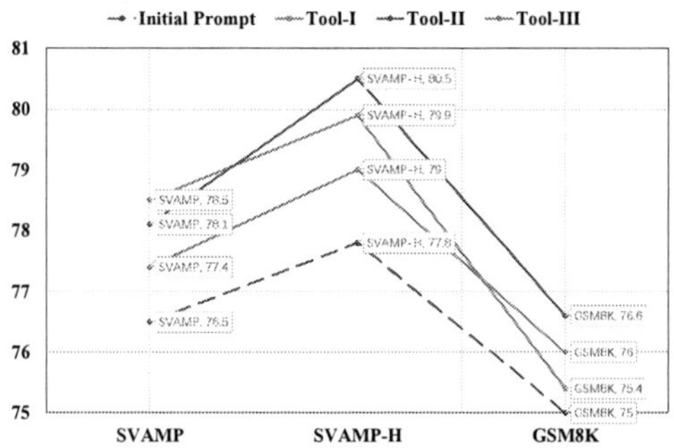

Figure 4: Model performances of different prompts. Here, we use the `gpt-3.5-turbo` as the backbone LLM.

ploration of *how to better utilize tools*, which involves a fusion of diverse solutions of LLMs and tool-augmented LLMs, culminating in the attainment of the final answer through tool-augmented interleaf prompting.

B Appendix A: Prompts

Table 7 presents COT prompts in our experiments. Table 8 shows three tool-based prompts obtained from our proposed self-prompt. It is worth noting that in most cases, the self-prompt does not alter the examples within the prompt. Its primary focus lies in modifying instructions related to tool usage, input-output formats, and tool definitions. All of them contain only 2 examples.

Table 9 shows the prompts of TIP in our experiments. Practically, we append "——" as the stopping symbols after each *Action* to achieve interleaving.

B.1 Definition of Self-consistency and Direct-Select

- COT-SC: Utilizing COT prompts in Table 1 for math reasoning and sampling 3 times.
- COT-SC: Utilizing tool-based prompts in Table 2 for math reasoning and sampling 3 times. Then we report their average results.
- Mix-SC: Selecting the most consistent answer from given options (A, B, C, D) in TIP.
- Directly Select: Select the answer from the given options in TIP through COT. Prompts are shown in Table 1.

C Appendix B: Self-Prompt

In this component, we conduct ablation studies to answer the question: How well do prompts from self-prompt perform? Figure 4 depicts a comparison between the initial tool-based prompt and the three prompts modified through self-prompt. It is evident across all three datasets that the prompts refined by self-prompt exhibit improved performance compared to the original initial prompts. This enhancement can be attributed to the provision of clearer, more explicit tool usage instructions and more standardized input-output formats. Overall, our self-prompt follows the road "LLMs know themselves better." The most simple implementation of self-prompt is to interact with ChatGPT or GPT-4 in OpenAI' website[2].

D Appendix C: More Cases

In this section, we present typical cases when IMR-TIP solves math reasoning tasks.

Table 10 presents the most straightforward scenario, wherein the provided solution corresponds with the answer generated by IMR-TIP in [Tho-2]. In this instance, the LLM detects the uniformity of all five answers upon comparison, resulting in a notable elevation of confidence and the subsequent direct issuance of the final answer.

Table 11 also provides an example wherein IMR-TIP makes an error. Instead of further comparing the reasoning steps of different solutions after analyzing the answers, the model directly presents a conclusion, asserting the correctness of its approach.

Table 12 introduces another intriguing case. In this instance, IMR-TIP attains the correct answer for [Tho-2]. However, upon reevaluating the preceding reasoning hints and formulas for [Tho-6], it identifies a numerical substitution error within [Tho-2]. Despite this recognition, IMR-TIP proceeds to output the identical formula as the final answer. Instances in which LLMs exhibit self-contradictory reasoning yet still yield the correct ultimate answer in IMR-TIP, as exemplified here, are referred to as "FALSE POSITIVE."

[2] chat.openai.com

COT prompts
Your task is to answer the following math questions. Question: julia played tag with 18 kids on monday . she played tag with 10 kids on Tuesday. how many more kids did she play with on monday than on Tuesday? Answer: Let's think step by step. julia playsed tag with 18 kids on monday and 10 kids tuesday, separately. So the amount of kids that she played with on monday than on tuesday is 18-10=8. So the answer is 8. Question: Jack had 9 action figures and 10 books on a shelf in his room. later he added 7 more action figures to the shelf. how many more action figures than books were on his shelf? Answer: Let's think step by step. The amount of action figures that Jack had is 9+7=16. And Jack had 10 books. So the amount of action figures than books on his shelf is 16-10=6. So the answer is 7.

Initial tool-based prompts
Your task is to solve the following middle-school arithmetic problems by using the Calculator. A calculator is a system used for performing mathematical calculations, ranging from basic arithmetic to more complex functions. You can do so by writing a mathematical equation and generating the answer format starting with "Answer = Calculator[expression]", where "expression" is the expression to be computed. Below are examples: Question: julia played tag with 18 kids on Monday. she played tag with 10 kids on Tuesday. how many more kids did she play with on monday than on Tuesday? Thought: The mathematical equation to solve the problem is: number of additional kids played with = number of kids played with on Monday - number of kids played with on Tuesday. Substituting the given values, we get: number of additional kids played with = 18 - 10. Therefore, Answer = Calculator[18 - 10] Question: Jack had 9 action figures and 10 books on a shelf in his room. later he added 7 more action figures to the shelf. how many more action figures than books were on his shelf? Thought: The mathematical equation to solve the problem is: difference in number of action figures and books = (number of action figures initially + number of action figures added) - number of books. Substituting the given values, we get: difference in number of action figures and books = (9 + 7) - 10. Therefore, Answer = Calculator[(9 + 7)- 10]

Direct-select prompts
There is a multiple choice question answering task. You are required to select one of the options to answer the problem. Let's think step by step.

Table 7: LLMs-COT, initial tool-based prompts and direct-select prompts in our experiments.

Prompt of Tool-I for math reasoning tasks.

Your task is to solve the following middle-school arithmetic problems using a calculator. Follow the steps provided to write out the algebraic and numeric equations, and use a calculator to find the answers. You can generate the answer format starting with "Answer = Calculator[expression]", where "expression" is the expression to be computed.
Example Problems:
Question: Julia played tag with 18 kids on Monday and 10 kids on Tuesday. How many more kids did she play with on Monday than on Tuesday?
Thought:
Algebraic Equation: Additional kids played with = Kids played with on Monday - Kids played with on Tuesday.
Numeric Equation: Additional kids played with = 18 - 10
Answer: Calculate Calculator[18 - 10]

Question : Jack had 9 action figures and 10 books on a shelf. Later, he added 7 more action figures to the shelf. How many more action figures than books were on his shelf?
Thought:
Algebraic Equation: Difference in action figures and books = (Initial action figures + Added action figures) - Number of books.
Numeric Equation: Difference in action figures and books = (9 + 7) - 10
Answer: Calculate Calculator[(9 + 7) - 10]
Remember to enter the appropriate equation into your calculator to find the answer. You can also explain how you would verify your solution.

Prompt of Tool-II for math reasoning tasks.

Your task is to solve the following middle-school arithmetic problems by using the Calculator. A calculator is a system used for performing mathematical calculations, ranging from basic arithmetic to more complex functions.

You can do so by writing out Algebraic Equation, Numeric Equation, Answer steps. In the Answer step, you should generate the output format with "Calculator[expression]", where "expression" is the expression to be computed.
Below are examples:
Question: julia played tag with 18 kids on monday. she played tag with 10 kids on Tuesday. how many more kids did she play with on monday than on Tuesday?
Thought: [Algebraic Equation]: number of additional kids played with = number of kids played with on Monday - number of kids played with on Tuesday.
[Numeric Equation]: number of additional kids played with = 18 - 10.
[Answer]: Calculator[18 - 10]

Question: Jack had 9 action figures and 10 books on a shelf in his room. later he added 7 more action figures to the shelf. how many more action figures than books were on his shelf?
Thought: [Algebraic Equation]: difference in number of action figures and books = (number of action figures initially + number of action figures added) - number of books.
[Numeric Equation]: difference in number of action figures and books = (9 + 7) - 10
[Answer]: Calculator[(9 + 7)- 10]

Prompt of Tool-III for math reasoning tasks.

Your task is to solve the following middle-school arithmetic problems by using the Calculator. A Calculator is a system used for performing mathematical calculations, ranging from basic arithmetic to more complex functions.

You can do so by writing out Algebraic Equation, Numeric Equation, and Answer steps:
(1) [Algebraic Equation], which directly builds an Algebraic Equation by using variables from the question to generate the solution.
(2) [Numeric Equation], which plugs in values from the question to transform the above Algebraic Equation into its numeric form.
(3) [Answer], which uses Calculator to calculate the above numeric equation, but not directly to give the final answer. You can generate the answer format with "Calculator[expression]", where "expression" is the expression to be computed.

Below are examples:
Question: julia played tag with 18 kids on monday. she played tag with 10 kids on tuesday. how many more kids did she play with on monday than on Tuesday?
Thought: [Algebraic Equation]: number of additional kids played with = number of kids played with on Monday - number of kids played with on Tuesday.
[Numeric Equation]: number of additional kids played with = 18 - 10.
[Answer]: Calculator[18 - 10]

Question: Jack had 9 action figures and 10 books on a shelf in his room. later he added 7 more action figures to the shelf. how many more action figures than books were on his shelf?
Thought: [Algebraic Equation]: difference in the number of figures and books = (number of figures initially + number of figures added) - number of books.
[Numeric Equation]: difference in the number of figures and books = (9 + 7) - 10
[Answer]: Calculator[(9 + 7)- 10]
You should keep in mind:
(1) you can not image or output the result of "Calculator[expression]".
(2) When generating a mathematical formula, do not include any units of measurement.

Table 8: Three tool-based prompts from Self-Prompt.

Your task is to validate the several options to the same math problem and select the correct ones. You should make your own reflections, revise your own thoughts, give the final answers based on the previous findings at the end. You can use the Calculator to help you calculate the numeric equations and verify the solutions.
A Calculator is a system used for performing mathematical calculations, ranging from basic arithmetic to more complex functions.
To do this, you can writing out interleaving Thought, Action and Answer steps. Notice that, you need to end with Answer when solving the task.
Below are examples:
Question: A robe takes 2287720 bolts of blue fiber and half that much white fiber. How many bolts in total does it take?
(A): A robe ...... 2287720 + (2287720/2) = 3,431,280 bolts.
(B): Based on the statement of the question ...... total number of bolts = Calculator[2287720 + (2287720/2)] = 3431580.
(C): [Algebraic Equation]: total number of bolts = number of blue bolts + number of white bolts...... Calculator[2287720 + (2287720 / 2)] = 3431580.
(D): [Algebraic Equation]: total number of bolts ......Calculator[2287720 + (2287720/2)] = 3431580.
Thoughts: [Thought-1]: To validate different solutions, I first need to analyze the math problem and give my reasoning logic.
[Action-1]: Analyze[problem]
[Thought-2]: First, the number of bolts of while fiber is half of the number of bolts of blue fiber. Total number of bolts = Number of bolts of blue fiber + Number of bolts of white fiber. Thus, total number of bolts = 2287720 + 2287720/2. To ensure the calculation is correct, I should use Caculator to calculate the answer.
[Action-2]: Calculator[2287720 + 2287720/2]
[Calculated Result]: 3431580
[Thought-3]: With the answer hint 3431580, I can first compare the answers of different options to make an initial assessment of their accuracy.
[Action-3]: Compare[answers]
[Thought-4]: The answer of option (A) is 3431280 that contradicts the answer hint 3431580, while options (B), (C), and (D) align with the answer hint. Therefore, I can preliminarily conclude that (A) is incorrect, and (B), (C), and (D) are correct. Since most of the answer options are consistent with my previous answer hint, I believe the current answer hint is likely correct. I can compare their reasoning steps and equations with mine to further verify my judgment and investigate why option (A) yielded an incorrect answer.
[Action-4]: Compare[reasoning]
[Thought-5]: Option (A) follows a similar reasoning process and formula as mine in [Thought-2], suggesting an error in the final calculation. Options (B), (C), and (D) provide equations that align with my earlier reasoning. Based on my findings, upon comparing the answers and reasoning processes, options (B), (C), and (D), along with the answer hint, are all correct.
[Answer]: Calculator[2287720 + 2287720/2]

Question: Trent is 5 years older than Jane, and Jane is 3 years younger than Quinn. If Quinn is 2538570, how old is Trent?
(A): Quinn is 2538570...... So the answer is Trent is 2538572.
(B): The mathematical equation to solve the problem is: ......Answer = Calculator[2538570 + (3 - 2538570) + 5] = 8.
(C): [Algebraic Equation]: Trent's age = Quinn's age ......2538578.
(D): [Algebraic Equation]: ...... Calculator[2538570 + 5 + 3] = 2538578.
Thoughts: [Thought-1]: To validate different solutions, I first need to analyze the math problem and give my reasoning logic.
[Action-1]: Analyze[problem]
[Thought-2]: I need to find Trent's age given the relationships between Trent, Jane, and Quinn's ages. Jane is 3 years younger than Quinn and 5 year younger than Trent. If Quinn is 2538570, Trent's age is 2538570 -3 + 5. To ensure the calculation is correct, I need to use Caculator to calculate the answer.
[Action-2]: Calculator[2538570 -3 + 5]
[Calculated Result]: 2538572
[Thought-3]: With the answer hint 2538572, I can frist compare the answers of different options to make an initial assessment of their accuracy.
[Action-3]: Compare[answers]
[Thought-4]: The answer of option (A) is 2538572 that align with the answer hint 2538572. However options (B)'s answer is 8, the answers of (C) and (D) are both 2538578 which all contradict the answer hint. Therefore, I can preliminarily conclude that (A) is correct, and (B), (C), and (D) are incorrect. But there are three different answers and only one aligns with the answer hint, I cannot determine which answer is definitely correct. Thus, I can compare their reasoning steps and equations with mine to further verify their correctness.
[Action-4]: Compare[reasoning]
[Thought-5]: (A) follows a similar reasoning process and formula as mine in [Thought-2]. (B) is correct in terms of the mathematical equation used, but the substitution is incorrect. It states that Jane's age is equal to 3. (C) and (D) present that Trent's age = Quinn's age + 8 (5+3), meaning that Trent is 5 years older that Jane, and Jane is 3 year older than Quinn which contradict the information given in the question. The correct algebraic equation would be to subtract 3 from Quinn's age to determine Jane's age and then add 5 to Jane's age to find Trent's age. Based on my findings, I think (B), (C) and (D) are wrong, the answer hint and (A) are correct with no need improvements. I don't need to review my previous answer hint.
[Answer]: Calculator[2538570 -3 + 5]

Question: Carla is downloading a 200 GB file. Normally she can download 2 GB/minute, but 40 percent of the way through the download, Windows forces a restart to install updates, which takes 20 minutes. Then Carla has to restart the download from the beginning. How load does it take to download the file?
(A): It will take her 200 minutes to download the file.
(B): The mathematical equation ...... Therefore, Answer = Calculator[(0.4 * (200/2)) + 20] = 60.
(C): [Algebraic Equation]: ...... Calculator[(200/2) + (200/2 * (1 - 0.4))/2] = 130.
(D): [Algebraic Equation]: total time ......[Answer]: Calculator[(200/2 + (200 - (200*0.4))/2) / 2] = 180.
Thoughts: [Thought-1]: To validate different solutions, I first need to analyze the math problem and give my reasoning logic.
[Action-1]: Analyze[problem]
[Thought-2]: First, I should list the equation to calculate the time it took Carla to download the data before the Windows restart: time before restart = Downloaded data/Download speed. And time after restart = File size/Donwload speed. Thus, the total time = time before restart + Windows update + time after restart. Thus, total time = 200 *0.4/2/2 + 20 + 200/2. To ensure the calculation is correct, I need to use Calculator to calculate the answer.
[Action-2]: Calculator[200 * 0.4/2/2 + 20 + 200/2]
[Calculated Result]: 140
[Thought-3]: With the answer hint 140, I can first compare the answers of different options to make an initial assessment of their accuracy.
[Action-3]: Compare[answers]
[Thought-4]: The answers of these options are 200, 60, 130 and 180, separately, that are different with the answer hint 140. Thus, I can not preliminarily conclude which one is correct. I need to further compare their reasoning steps and equations with mine to further verify their correctness.
[Action-4]: Compare[reasoning]
[Thought-5]: (B), (C), and (D) have flawed algebraic equations as they omit the inclusion of Windows update time mentioned in the reasoning hint. (A) lacks reasoning steps, making its correctness uncertain. Because none options have the same answer as mine, I need to review [Thought-2] again to validate the accuracy of my previous reasoning and answer hint.
[Action-5]: Rethink[Thought-2]
[Thought-6]: The algebraic equation in [Thought-2] is correct, but the substitution is incorrect. The correct total time = 200 *0.4/2 + 20 + 200/2 rather than 200 *0.4/2/2 + 20 + 200/2. So based on my findings, the answer is Calculator[200 * 0.4/2 + 20 + 200/2].
[Answer]: Calculator[200 * 0.4/2 + 20 + 200/2]

Keep in mind the following requirements:
(1) You must output the correct equation as the final answer in [Answer].
(2) If answers of all options are the same as the answer hint, you can directly end the task and output the correct equation in Answer.
(3) If you decide to use Calculator in Action, generate the format with "Calculator[expression]", where "expression" is the expression to be computed.
(4) Do not include any units of measurement in "Calculator[expression]".
(5) You can not image the results of "Calculator[expression]".

Table 9: Prompts of TIP. In this table, we omit details of each option.

Question: There were some birds sitting on the fence. 725067 more birds came to join them. if there are a total of 544650 birds on the fence now how many birds had been sitting on the fence at the start?
(A): The total number of birds on the fence now is 544650. And 725067 more birds came to join them. So the total number of birds at the start is 544650 - 725067 = -180417.
(B): Answer = Calculator[544650 - 725067] = -180417
(C): [Algebraic Equation]: number of birds at the start = total number of birds on the fence now - number of birds that came to join them. [Numeric Equation]: number of birds at the start = 544650 - 725067 [Answer]: Calculator[544650 - 725067] = -180417
(D): [Algebraic Equation]: number of birds at the start = total number of birds on the fence now - number of birds that came to join them. [Numeric Equation]: number of birds at the start = 544650 - 725067 [Answer]: Calculator[544650 - 725067] = -180417

IMR-TIP:
Tho-1: To validate different solutions, I first need to analyze the math problem and give my reasoning logic.
Act-1: Analyze[problem]
Tho-2: The problem states that there were some birds sitting on the fence, and 725067 more birds came to join them. The total number of birds on the fence now is 544650. To find the number of birds that had been sitting on the fence at the start, we can subtract the number of birds that came to join from the total number of birds now. To ensure the calculation is correct, I need to use the Calculator to calculate the answer.
Act-2: Calculator[544650 - 725067]
Tho-3: With the answer hint -180417, I can first compare the answers of different options to make an initial assessment of their accuracy.
Act-3: Compare[answers]
Tho-4: The answers of options (A), (B), (C), and (D) are all -180417, which align with the answer hint -180417. Therefore, I can conclude that all options are correct. No more action are needed.
Ans: **-180417.0**

Ground-Truth Anaswer: **-180417.0**

Table 10: The MOST SIMPLE interleaved example of generated solutions by IMR-TIP on SVAMP-Hard dataset.

Question: julia played tag with 829557 kids on monday and 853729 kids on tuesday. she played cards wtih 913524 kids on Wednesday. how many kids did she play tag with altogether?
(A): Julia played tag with 829,557 kids on Monday and 853,729 kids on Tuesday. To find out how many kids she played tag with altogether, we need to add these two numbers together. 829,557 + 853,729 = 1,683,286 So, Julia played tag with a total of 1,683,286 kids altogether.
(B): Answer = Calculator[829557 + 853729] = 1683286
(C): [Algebraic Equation]: total number of kids played tag with = number of kids played tag with on Monday + number of kids played tag with on Tuesday + number of kids played tag with on Wednesday. [Numeric Equation]: total number of kids played tag with = 829557 + 853729 + 913524 [Answer]: Calculator[829557 + 853729 + 913524] = 2596810
(D): [Algebraic Equation]: total number of kids played tag with = number of kids played tag with on Monday + number of kids played tag with on Tuesday + number of kids played tag with on Wednesday. [Numeric Equation]: total number of kids played tag with = 829557 + 853729 + 913524 [Answer]: Calculator[829557 + 853729 + 913524] = 2596810

IMR-TIP:
Tho-1: To validate different solutions, I first need to analyze the math problem and give my reasoning logic.
Act-1: Analyze[problem]
Tho-2: Julia played tag with a certain number of kids on Monday, Tuesday, and Wednesday. To find out how many kids she played tag with altogether, I need to add the number of kids she played tag with on each day. The equation to calculate the total number of kids played tag with is: total number of kids played tag with = number of kids played tag with on Monday + number of kids played tag with on Tuesday + number of kids played tag with on Wednesday. To ensure the calculation is correct, I need to use the Calculator to calculate the answer.
Act-2: Calculator[829557 + 853729 + 913524]
Tho-3: With the answer hint 2596810, I can first compare the answers of different options to make an initial assessment of their accuracy.
Act-3: Compare[answers]
Tho-4: The answers of options (A), (B), (C), and (D) are 1,683,286, 1,683,286, 2,596,810, and 2,596,810, respectively. The answer hint is 2,596,810. Therefore, options (A) and (B) are incorrect, while options (C) and (D) are correct. Since options (C) and (D) have the same answer and reasoning process, I can conclude that the correct answer is Calculator[829557 + 853729 + 913524].
Ans: **2596810**

Ground-Truth Anaswer: **1683286.0**

Table 11: The typical NEGATIVE interleaved example of generated solutions by IMR-TIP on SVAMP-Hard dataset.

Question: Sadie slept 8 hours on Monday. For next two days, she slept 2 hours less, each, because she had to complete some assignments. If the rest of the week she slept 1 hour more than those two days, how many hours did she sleep in total throughout the week?
(A): Wendi feeds each of her chickens three cups of mixed chicken feed, containing seeds, mealworms and vegetables to help keep them healthy. So the amount of cups of feed that Wendi needs to give her chickens in the final meal of the day is 20x3=60. So the answer is 60.
(B): The mathematical equation to solve the problem is: total cups of feed = (number of chickens * cups of feed per meal) - (cups of feed given in morning + cups of feed given in afternoon). Substituting the given values, we get: total cups of feed = (20 * 3) - (6887483 + 25). Therefore, Answer = Calculator[(20 * 3) - (6887483 + 25)] = -6887448.
(C): [Algebraic Equation]: number of cups of feed for the final meal = (number of chickens * cups of feed per chicken) - (cups of feed given in the morning + cups of feed given in the afternoon). [Numeric Equation]: number of cups of feed for the final meal = (20 * 3) - (6887483 + 25) [Answer]: Calculator[(20 * 3) - (6887483 + 25)] =-6887448
(D): [Algebraic Equation]: total cups of feed for the final meal = (number of chickens * cups of feed per chicken) - (cups of feed given in the morning + cups of feed given in the afternoon) [Numeric Equation]: total cups of feed for the final meal = (20 * 3) - (6887483 + 25) [Answer]: Calculator[(20 * 3) - (6887483 + 25)] = -6887448

IMR-TIP:
Tho-1: To validate different solutions, I first need to analyze the math problem and give my reasoning logic.
Act-1: Analyze[problem]
Tho-2: Wendi needs to give her chickens three cups of feed in three separate meals. She has already given 6887483 cups of feed in the morning and 25 cups of feed in the afternoon. Thus, the number of cups of feed that Wendi needs to give her chickens in the final meal of the day is (Number of chickens * Cups of feed per chicken) - (Cups of feed given in the morning + Cups of feed given in the afternoon). To ensure the calculation is correct, I need to use Calculator to calculate the answer.
Act-2: **Calculator[(20 * 3) - (6887483 + 25)]**
Tho-3: With the answer hint -6887448, I can first compare the answers of different options to make an initial assessment of their accuracy.
Act-3: Compare[answers]
Tho-4: **The answers of these options are 60, -6887448, -6887448 and -6887448, separately, which are different with the answer hint -6887448.** Thus, I can not preliminarily conclude which one is correct. I need to further compare their reasoning steps and equations with mine to further verify their correctness.
Act-4: Compare[reasoning]
Tho-5: Option (A) follows a similar reasoning process as mine in [Tho-2], but the equation is incorrect. Options (B), (C), and (D) provide equations that align with my earlier reasoning. However, the substitution is incorrect as it does not include the cups of feed given in the morning and afternoon. Based on my findings, upon comparing the answers and reasoning processes, options (A), (B), (C), and (D) are all incorrect. I need to review [Tho-2] again to validate the accuracy of my previous reasoning and answer hint.
Act-5: Rethink[Tho-2].
Tho-6: The algebraic equation in [Tho-2] is correct, but the substitution is incorrect. The correct total cups of feed = (Number of chickens * Cups of feed per chicken) - (Cups of feed given in the morning + Cups of feed given in the afternoon). **So based on my findings, the answer is Calculator[(20 * 3) - (6887483 + 25)].**
Act-6: Calculator[(20 * 3) - (6887483 + 25)]
Ans: **-6887448**

Ground-Truth Anaswer: **-6887448**

Table 12: FALSE POSITIVE Examples of generated solutions by IMR-TIP on GSM8K-Hard dataset.

Author Index

Association for Computational Linguistics
209 N. Eighth Street
Stroudsburg, Pennsylvania 18360

ISBN 979-8-3313-0172-9

CURRAN ASSOCIATES INC.
proceedings.com

25th Annual Conference of the European Association for Machine Translation (EAMT 2024)

Volume 2: Products & Projects

Sheffield, United Kingdom
24 – 27 June 2024